Champions Never Tell

Sisters Surviving Storms In The Workplace

By Jil Jordan Greene and Christy Rutherford

Featuring – Cheryl Snapp Conner, Dr. Valorie Parker-Hagan,
Jade Brown Russell, Ronetta Francis, VonGretchen Nelson

Champions Never Tell

First Edition for Print November 2017

Book Cover created by Michelle Washington – Women of More Magazine

Special Thanks to Johnny Mack – Span Books for Consultation and Guidance www.spanbooks.com

ISBN-13: 978-0692979969

ISBN-10: 0692979964

Thank You

God, for sheltering us through our storms and then using them to unleash our greatness to serve others.

Our families for unconditional love and support.

The tyrants, bullies, naysayers and bystanders. Without your crushing, we wouldn't have known how strong we were. You thought you set us up for failure, but you released us to our destinies. We forgive you and are forever grateful.

Table of Contents

Foreword

As a woman, I'm sure you've heard the adage that you need to work twice as hard as your male counterparts to succeed. So, you play the game hoping to be rewarded for your hard work and personal sacrifice. Now, you're up for that well-deserved promotion, long overdue special assignment, or some other professional breakthrough – finally, it's your time.

It's at this point that many women in the workplace experience the "glass ceiling." It becomes painfully clear that playing by "their rules" isn't enough because they change the rules on you in a heartbeat. Women have to constantly maneuver those moving goal posts countless times each day in the American workplace. For Jil Jordan Greene, Christy Rutherford, Cheryl Snapp Connor, Dr. Valorie Parker-Hagan, Jade Brown Russell, Ronetta Francis and VonGretchen Nelson, the moving goal posts were a continuous trial in countless situations.

Far too many women in the workplace face a set of dynamics that are unique to being a woman in a traditionally white, male-dominated world. In this landmark book, the authors share their personal stories to explain how leadership experiences for women are radically different from those of their male counterparts. These differences, according to the authors, lead to miscues, distortion in communications, and often get in the way of optimal performance and personal job satisfaction.

Champions Never Tell, helps make the invisible visible by using real workplace situations and stories to explore the assumptions that cause misunderstandings between women leaders and those who work with them. The authors provide specific recommendations on how to identify and respond to difficult situations.

The book's most powerful impact comes from the specific advice to women leaders on how to become more competent, confident and comfortable confronting individuals in the workplace who harass, bully, intimidate, discriminate or retaliate against women because of their gender.

The authors explore the ideals and realities of gender, meritocracy, opportunity, and disparate treatment that is a constant in our world. More notably, the book lays out 31 concrete strategies to help women survive and thrive in the workplace. The strategies will help advance women to the next level of personal and professional success, and unleash the greatness that lies within.

Thanks to the courage, authenticity, and transparency of the authors, women reading this book will:

- Learn how to use their gender as an asset
- Expand beyond their comfort zone
- Recognize and demonstrate excellence
- Build mutually beneficial relationships and nurturing networks
- Identify powerful mentors and learn from their experiences
- Discover ways of working with others to achieve desired outcomes

Champions Never Tell shows how women professionals can (and must) think, and act both courageously and boldly. To combine the strength of their peers with the wisdom of their mentors, and fight the fights that need fighting – and WIN!

I have been a human resource professional for over two decades. My specialty is diversity management - specifically helping people around the corner and around the world understand the inherent dignity of individuals, and help organizations get the optimum talent from all people. I have been greatly influenced by the diversity work I conduct, and have seen the power of diversity within companies, communities, and the country.

It is time for men to start having honest and meaningful discussions about gender equity, which is desperately needed to reach a different level of acceptance and understanding required to deconstruct institutional sexism and sex discrimination in our workplace. The first step is to understand the concept and impact of male privilege.

We can't have it both ways. We can't say that we want an honest discussion about gender equity, but when Terry O'Neil from the National Organization for Women talks about advancing feminism as a counterbalance against male privilege, we immediately write her off, call her sexist and unenlightened. We must be honest and understand that men can't pretend not to be affected by all of what the authors of, *Champions Never Tell* have so passionately described in this book.

At some point, I must figure out how to use my position of male privilege to create fairness and respect for women in my company, in my community, and yes, in this country. More importantly, I must convince other men to also do this with the understanding that there may be consequences for going against the grain. I personally believe it is time for men like me - Diversity Officers - to "Do Our Damn Job" and eliminate or manage bias and privilege in the workplace.

I am honored to be a part of this landmark book and look forward to the open and honest conversations that come as a result of these amazing authors openly sharing their stories to provide much needed healing to women leaders around the world.

Shelton J. Goode, DPA
Chief Compliance Officer and Executive Director, Diversity and Inclusion for the Metropolitan Atlanta Rapid Transit Authority and author of *Crisis as a Platform for Social Change from Strawberry Mansion to Silicon Valley*

Preface

From the beginning, we would like to set the tone for this book. This book isn't intended to discredit an organization, male bash, name call or portray women as victims. The intention of this book is to highlight and illuminate issues that are pervasive in organizations domestically and globally. We intend to share healing information with women who are knowingly and unknowingly, in toxic or hostile work environments.

Champions Never Tell features a unique group of women from diverse backgrounds, industries and careers. We are coming together on purpose to show that we can create a better future for women in the workplace, and positively impact and increase the number of women in the pipeline for executive level positions. Through open and honest conversations, we can create change in workplaces and homes.

Regardless of race/ethnicity, background, industry (nursing, lawyers, IT, telecommunications, finance, coal mining, professors, military, doctors, etc.), ambitious women from around the world share a large number of commonalities.

We share similar stories of pain from having a large number of critics, unhealed wounds, baggage we carry, guilty about not having balance, and the secret desires that go untapped. Adding these issues to all the battles we fight to ascend the ladder of success is exhausting, so by the time we reach the top, it doesn't feel like success. We don't feel successful, because we are bleeding from all the battle scars. This is not true for all women, but it's true for many of us.

Adding a hostile or toxic work environment on top of everything that it takes to succeed can make going to work each day unbearable. When it comes to women being harassed, the media is reporting the information in silos. Stating it's women in tech, women in the military, women in Muslim countries, or women in male dominated industries (firefighters, police), etc.

The media also tends to solely focus on sexual harassment, which is the least form of harassment. Hostile engagements and racial discrimination are actually more common, but are the least talked about.

There are countless women suffering from harassment in their work environment, but are reluctant to report it. The lack of awareness creates situations where women are unsure of whether or not they're victims of gender discrimination. There is a stigma around being classified a victim, so many women suffer in silence.

Not only are women reluctant to report it, some women are reluctant to even acknowledge they are being harassed. Many women deny it, even when it is objectively true. [i] They are unwilling to see the obvious, because if they see it for what it is, they feel they would have to claim victim status, and CHAMPIONS are never victims.

Since women are reluctant to open up and don't have common stories or conversations about it, they are suffering silently. The silence erupts in disease, mental illness, broken homes, divorces, and a host of countless issues that women face alone.

In this book, we would like to put stories and faces behind the suffering. We would like to let women know that they are not alone in uncomfortable situations that they face. We would like to let women know that they can choose a different path. They have the option to take action and make the necessary decisions to preserve their mental and physical health and be there for their families in the way they intended.

The Untold Battles

It has been proven, time and time again, that companies and organizations with women in senior leadership positions perform better. Women comprise more than half of all college graduates, and nearly 40 percent of MBAs, but only represent 6 percent of Fortune 500 CEOs[ii] and 11 percent of board members.[iii]

Earlier in 2017, Ursula Burns resigned as the CEO of Xerox, and Rosalind Brewer as CEO of Sam's Club, leaving a gap where there are no African American women represented as CEO's of Fortune 500 companies. Also, African American women make up less than two percent of middle managers, which comes from a pipeline created that will feed the C-suite.

Companies have spent millions of dollars, and expended just as many hours, studying the large gap between women in senior leadership positions and the number that graduate from college and enter the workforce. They want to understand why there is a gap, where women lose momentum, what causes women to leave, and how to increase the numbers in executive leadership. These studies have drawn a wide range of conclusions, observations, speculations, and recommendations.

With the increased racial tension in the U.S., companies are investing heavily in diversity programs, unconscious bias training, diversity and inclusion training, and a whole host of efforts to ease the conversation about our differences. Although some of these efforts may be marginally effective, they won't have as much impact if there isn't buy-in and outward support from the executive leaders.

A McKinsey study stated, "The difference between committed CEOs and others is subtle...hands on CEOs reach out to get other senior male leaders involved in the effort, making them catalysts for change."[iv] With the rise in the ousting of CEO's from companies who fail to address hostile work environments, like UBER, it takes a lot more than "hosting training sessions" for the sake of training.

Also, in the case of Harvey Weinstein who used his power in an industry to engage in heinous acts against scores of women, there has to be an expectation of a *culture shift,* and this is the unspoken gap that needs to be highlighted and addressed.

Having a diversity program to recruit highly qualified minorities and/or women into organizations is a great initiative. However, inviting a small group of diverse individuals into a majority culture that does not see the need for change, nor desire it, the unintended consequences of not addressing the *culture* will result in a hostile work environment for a program intended for good-will.

Instead of setting new expectations, having tough conversations and holding people accountable for misconduct, organizations are masking the issues with "diversity training." However, without passionate buy-in from the executive level, people view diversity training as an escape from work or their heavy workload. It's a good break or a chance to be off-site away from the office, with coffee, pastries, and a free lunch, but is it effective?

Are organizations really focused on the results of the training or are they just checking the box, because the *intention* of the training will drive the results. People know the difference and will tolerate the training because they have to be there, but not because there's an expectation of organizational change.

Organizations are expanding and adding roles for Diversity and Inclusion Directors, Civil Rights personnel, Equal Employment Opportunity (EEO), but depending on where they are placed within the organization and the *intention* of their roles, many of these positions quickly become ornamental and ineffective.

McKinsey also noted, "Successful companies appoint well-respected managers to shine the spotlight on diversity issues and help maintain cycle after cycle..." The only way you change unacceptable behavior is to call it out and make sure there are consequences to make the individual stop acting that way. This takes courage, but it also takes clout."[v]

In organizations that lack diversity at the executive level, there is an unspoken, but highly visible resistance to the idea of having a diverse executive suite. From experience, many women and minorities feel that their organization is fond of a non-diverse boardroom, and the executive leaders make it their mission to keep it that way.

Women Are Neutralized Early In Their Careers

The way that women and/or minorities are treated in the workplace stems from a majority member's experience with that type of person. It also comes from the majority member's culture and background. If the majority member doesn't have personal experience with minorities, they revert to what's depicted on television and described in the media. There are tons of stereotypes floating around for each minority group, and that sets the minority up for a host of challenges to overcome for themselves and the people they work for.

Women are considered minorities in some organizations and industries, especially in science, technology, engineering and math (STEM). Minority women are **double minorities** and are commonly subjected to a host of stereotypes. White women share the commonality of being white with the majority (white men). Men of color share the commonality of being men, with white men. Women of color don't share a commonality, and have more work to do when it comes to closing the gap.

Many women lose their ambition and become discouraged within the first two years of their career. A Bain study found that in the first two years of a person's career, more women aspired to executive levels and were more confident than men. However, after two or more years into their career, women's aspirations plummet by 60 percent and confidence by nearly 50 percent, while men's aspirations remained the same, and their confidence declined by only 10 percent.[vi]

Ambitious women are targeted and neutralized early in their careers. This constitutes the lack of highly qualified women ascending up the pipeline to executive level positions. If the first few years are formative and builds a strong foundation for a successful career, then why are women falling through the cracks?

This highlights the fact that if organizations want to build a highly qualified pipeline of women leaders, they need to start very early in a young woman's career. When women are treated well, with respect, given meaningful work and mentored, they have a greater opportunity to excel. Having access and exposure to other high-level women is a bonus, but not required to be successful in the formative years.

Women can also have terrible experiences in their first two years and still thrive. The study mentioned above is not a catchall for women, but illustrate the foundational years of a woman's career are important.

When it comes to black women, they are 2.8 times as likely to aspire to powerful and prestigious titles compared to white women, but report feeling stalled, and that their talents go unrecognized by supervisors. Black women also find it difficult to win sponsorship, where only 11 percent had sponsors.[vii] This is a major problem and barrier to success, because 90 percent of executive level women at 60 major corporations attribute their success to having significant sponsorship. [viii]

When met with challenges, women who are looking to excel at all costs, rarely say that they are having issues because of their gender or race/ethnicity. Ambitious women are unlikely to blame being mistreated because they are women or double minorities, because if they say that, they feel victimized. Ambitious women *will never* claim victim status. That would be taking a lower position and settling for a fate that was not in their hands. Ambitious women will find other ways to excel, and chalk it up to the game to move forward and do whatever it takes to succeed.

Workplace Bullying

A common issue, not widely talked about or studied, is workplace bullying. It is the repeated and unreasonable actions of individuals (or a group) directed towards an employee (or a group of employees) intended to humiliate, intimidate, degrade, or undermine, which creates risk to the health or safety of the employee.[ix]

Workplace bullies are often in supervisory and/or managerial roles, and nearly 35 percent of Americans have experienced one. Since there is a general lack of awareness about workplace bullying and an element of personal shame involved, people don't realize they are victims and are reluctant to report it. The lack of awareness also keeps companies/organizations from addressing it properly.

Workplace bullying has hurt more employees than sexual harassment, and nearly half of the people targeted suffer stress-related health conditions, which include debilitating anxiety, an impaired immune system, post-traumatic stress disorder (PTSD), and cardiovascular problems.[x]

According to the 2014 Workplace Bullying Institute Survey:[xi]
- Most bullies are men (69 percent) and target mostly women
- Women bullies (31 percent) target other women 2 times higher than they do men
- Women bully other women at a higher rate than men bully women
- Nearly 80 percent of women who are bullied by men lose their jobs
- Nearly 90 percent of women who are bullied by women lose their jobs
- When men bully women, they lose their jobs at a lower rate than when they bully men
- When women bully men, they lose their jobs at a higher rate than when they bully other women

Who Is The Book For?

This book is for women who are confused about what may be going on in their workplace. It's for women who are at their wits end about being mistreated. It's for women who want to know that they are not alone, and are not over reacting.

Staying in hostile work environments for long periods of time can cause emotional trauma and scars that last a lifetime. The trauma is magnified when organizations continue to promote toxic leaders and allow mistreatment, regardless of how many people's careers are affected and destroyed.

Our intention in this book is to offer guidance and insight to provide clarity to women who are looking for answers. We hope that our willingness to be vulnerable and share our stories will allow women to see themselves honestly and then choose to do something different. While many women are waiting for their organizations or industries to advocate for them on their behalf, they are waiting in vain and are continuously disappointed.

It's time to take a new approach and not only ask what organizations are doing, but to look in the mirror and ask what can be done individually, starting with the woman in the mirror.

This book also provides insight to organizations that really want to effect change, but can't identify the gaps in what they need to do. We hope that this book will offer love and healing to strengthen the Mental, Physical and Spiritual Health of women around the world, who are suffering in hostile and toxic work environments.

Proceeds from this book benefit Hurricane Relief Efforts. We would like to support families who have been devastated by the recent hurricanes and understand that it takes years to fully recover. While the world may have shifted their attention, we'd like to do our part in supporting the efforts to restore families back to their standard of living.

Like our Facebook page and join a community of like-minded women who are ready to shift their life for the best. Stay up to date on our upcoming events, retreats and get connected with accountability partners for the work outlined in the Appendix.

To Your Success!! www.facebook.com/championsnevertell

Chapter 1

Exposing The Invisible
By Christy Rutherford

The Equal Employment Opportunity Commission defines harassment as unwelcome conduct that is based on race, color, religion, sex (including pregnancy), national origin, age (40 or older), disability or genetic information. Harassment becomes unlawful when:

1) enduring the offensive conduct becomes a condition of continued employment, or

2) the conduct is severe or pervasive enough to create a work environment that a reasonable person would consider intimidating, hostile, or abusive.

However, petty slights, annoyances, and isolated incidents do not rise to the level of being illegal. The conduct must create a work environment that would be intimidating, hostile, or offensive to reasonable people for it to be illegal.

The petty slights and isolated incidents are micro-aggressions and subtle attacks that occur over a long period of time. These incidents are more common and stay below the line of illegal harassment, but the effects it can have on someone's health and job are detrimental. Not being able to pinpoint exactly what types of non-blatant acts are considered harassment, and witnessing the swift and unjust retaliation upon women who filed complaints, also keeps women from reporting it.

The ladies featured in this book share their stories of being harassed by a wide range of people, which make up different ethnicities and genders. While the stories are real, the names have been changed or characters altered (three people in one) to protect the brands of the organizations depicted. We're still looking to hold our former organizations in high integrity, even if they didn't ensure the same for us.

Are Black Women Considered Invisible?

To "assimilate" is to conform or adjust to the customs, attitudes of a group, nation or the like. Black women want to be seen for our contributions, regardless of race or gender, and in order to be successful, taken seriously and considered a counterpart, some of us consciously and unconsciously assimilate into the culture of the majority. In a number of industries and organizations in the U.S., the majority is white men.

Nearly 10 years into my career, Dr. Michael Eric Dyson talked about assimilation at a diversity summit. Although I couldn't articulate exactly why I didn't FEEL as successful as my position, income and awards reflected, Dr. Dyson made me realize that I assimilated in my organization's culture to fit in and be successful. What a revelation! I consciously and unconsciously downplayed my culture, femininity, and preferences in order to fit into the majority culture.

Over time, this had a tremendous impact on my self-image and being authentic about who I was at my core. It also created a great imbalance when it came to achieving just as much success in my personal life as I had in my professional life.

At work, it was exhausting and confusing to try to strike a balance between too much femininity and too little masculinity. With my family, it created a host of challenges because I no longer ate the same food from my southern roots. Taking hummus and cream cheese pinwheels to family functions were not well received. AT ALL.....EVER!

The disappointing thing about losing a sense of self and family by assimilating to fit into the workplace and have high levels of success is, regardless of the sacrifice, leaders still tend to hire and promote people who look like them, and who have similar backgrounds and careers.[xii] This becomes more and more apparent in higher levels of leadership.

Assimilation may be a reason why some white male executives claim they don't see race or gender when they see black women. They say they just see colleagues. Is this true? If we're assimilating and have the chameleon effect in order to fit in, they may not see us for who we are. They see us for who we pretend to be in order to get along and effectively do our jobs.

When we awaken to this, and realize we've given up so much but still can't seem to get past unseen barriers, it creates guilt, shame, and resentment. We don't know that millions of other women have done the same thing consciously and unconsciously to succeed. An interesting study revealed that black women were more likely to go unnoticed in a crowd. They showed a group of white participants a series of photos depicting black and white men and women. Later, they showed the participants a new set of photos, while mixing in some of the old. They found that the participants had a harder time remembering whether or not they had seen the black women's faces before, compared to the other groups, including black men. The exercise suggested that black women were more likely to go unnoticed in a social setting or group.

They also tested whether black women were likely to go unheard when contributing to group conversations. Using a group of eight people, including two black and white men and women. The white participants were asked to observe their conversation.

Once finished, they were given a list of comments and asked to match the comments with the speaker. The results revealed they made the most errors when identifying the comments between the two black women, suggesting the two women were interchangeable and not individuals.

Also, they misattributed the black women's comments to other speakers in the group, indicating that black women were more likely to go unheard to a largely white audience, and their comments and suggestions are attributed to other people in the room.[xiii]
Wow!

Why Do We Stay?

Two years ago, someone asked a group of women in leadership positions on LinkedIn, "Why do you stay at a job you hate?" With over 200 comments, most women said they stayed because they built their lifestyle around their income, and couldn't afford to leave. Some simply said, "Golden Handcuffs."

Knowing there is a greater and brighter future available to ambitious women, I was saddened by the comments. There are so many women that write off the best part of their lives, and are unwilling to do anything about it. *Is this you?*

Reflecting on my own career and what I've learned from other ambitious women, these are a few reasons why most women stay in jobs we hate.

We Finally Achieved Our Goal. When I finally achieved the level of success that I worked so hard for and got my seat at the executive table, it wasn't what I expected. Nightmare on Elm Street started every morning at 8am, and I hated going to the morning meetings that I longed to go to earlier in my career. I was the only woman in the room and didn't expect to have as much resistance once I finally earned the seat. I thought that the fight ended when I got in the room, but the true battle had just begun. I had to defend that seat every single day.

Some ambitious women believe that a career fiercely won is worth dying for. It stops being about what's best for us, and becomes about not giving up after finally winning. Some women are also trapped in jobs, because of the expectations of other people. Since we finally got what we wanted, we don't feel like we can tell anyone that we are unfulfilled since they all admire what we've achieved.

We are Super Heroes to many. We represent women in our organization, women of similar ethnicity or women of color. We are heroes to our families, friends, associates, and colleagues in our respective industries. When people see us at or near the top, they see our cape. However, they don't see that the very cape that we use to save and inspire others has become wrapped around our necks, and choking us to death.

We got what we always wanted, but get choked out daily with all of the unintended consequences of achieving high levels of success. We mask the pain with wine, paint a smile on our faces, and dress it all up with expensive clothing, but we suffer.... silently...because no one REALLY wants to hear that their super hero is actually H-U-M-A-N.

When we remain silent, we get caught in the cycle of the 9-5 life, and lose sight of becoming who we dreamed of. We get comfortable being uncomfortable, and write off our dreams to stay in positions we bled for.

The Pay Affords An Incredible Lifestyle - I lived on a golf course, bought two houses before I was 28. I had my dream car, and traveled at least twice a month. I was living the life that people dreamed of, so how dare I admit to being unhappy?

Who would listen anyway? My family, who were so proud of my achievements? My friends? They knew, because they were unhappy too, and we regularly shared our stories around alcoholic beverages at our favorite Happy Hour spot, or on exotic vacations. One day, I realized the money wasn't worth my unhappiness.

When we live a life that people admire, we aren't allowed to be unhappy about it. Some women hold on to toxic jobs to maintain a mortgage or an expensive car in an effort to "show" how successful they are. Suddenly they are trapped in the job, because they have to work to keep their standard of living. Also, keeping a job for the great medical benefits, when the job is creating the severe medical conditions that require treatment.

You Can't Change If You Don't Feel. Five years ago, I was a walking pincushion with a hardened heart. I had more knives in my back than a steak house. Ascending up the ladder of success, fighting battles and the general "whooping" that life put on me. I found that I was numb to a life that once felt amazing.

There are trade-offs to high levels of success. Many women know they are numb, but don't know what to do about it or how to change it. A lot of us put up walls to protect ourselves from the pain

5

of life, but this also keeps out the good. Energy flows both ways, and walls can suffocate you and the dreams you had for your life.

How To Use This Book

The purpose of this book is to allow you to see some of the subtle and unconscious ways women are treated in the workplace. We want to provide you with a mirror that will allow you to reflect your current reality and then, expand your awareness for how it affects your overall quality of life, and to determine if you feel you are in a hostile/toxic work environment.

We share insight, recommendations, and action steps that you can take to restore your mental, physical and spiritual wellness. In the Appendix, there's a checklist associated with 31 action steps, so you can track what you're doing and how you feel over time.

To assist you with reflecting on your progress, there's a set of questions that will allow you to see where you are now and quarterly. If you're working and following the steps in this book for 6-8 months and your reality isn't changing, it should give you a clear picture of your quality of life, and the courage to seek other opportunities.

First Step - Go to the Appendix of this book. Fill out the Day 1 Wholeness Check Sheet, and assess where you are in this moment.

Second - Scroll through Days 1-31 and take a look at the keys we've offered for your mental, physical, spiritual wellness and wholeness.

Third –Start with the action listed on the day of the month that you start. If you start on November 15th, go to Offering 15. This makes it easier to track your progress monthly. Put a check in the box to track it and then, repeat the same for each subsequent day. Repeat the same each month for a year. We want you to start your journey to healing before reading the book as it may take some time to finish. Start with the end in mind.

Forth - Read the stories of the ladies in this book and see if you share commonalities. Use them to illuminate and give meaning to some of the things you may be feeling. Forgive yourself for not knowing, and also, never ever ever claim to be a victim. Les Brown said, "Victims are powerless. You are powerful!"

Fifth – After three months, track your progress, where you are and then, answer the questions in the Quarterly Reflection.

Lastly – Give yourself permission to be happy, healthy, whole and loved. You DESERVE it! You are WORTH it! You are a CHAMPION!

Chapter 2

The Devil Wears ~~Prada~~ Navy Blue
By Jil Jordan Greene

"There is a special place in hell for women who don't help each other!" ~ Madeleine Albright

The Devil Wears Navy Blue is a story about a young rising professional navigating her way through corporate America. She encountered three different types of workplace storms that at some point, most women experience today. The storms captured here are demonstrated through hostile working environment, workplace harassment, sexual harassment, invisible syndrome, and sabotage.

STORM #1

I sat in a small but very nice office waiting for the hiring manager to come in to conduct my final interview. The beautiful mahogany desk stared at me, as I envisioned sitting behind it. The door opened and in walked a very sharp, tall polished woman. She had long shoulder length red hair, what appeared to be a custom-made navy blue suit, and shiny leather navy blue heels. I could feel the breeze as she moved past me in the office, which was an indication that she was rushing and in a hurry.

I learned she was a senior executive in the company, and the one who I would report to. I will call her 'Mrs. Navy Blue' because I learned that she wore navy blue every day to the office. The thought of working for her was exciting. I dreamed about working for a successful powerful woman. Working for someone who could teach me how to successfully climb the corporate ladder. I looked forward to someone who would mentor me.

According to the Harvard Business Review, 72 percent of men who receive mentorship and support from other men get a promotion within two years, so I was looking forward to similar results.

As our interview came to an end, I felt good. I knew Mrs. Navy Blue was going to hire me. Her last question was an omen, and I just didn't know it. She said, "Have you ever had a bad boss?"

Rising Star

I received the offer for the job and was thrilled. My two years were full of wins and recognition, and life was great. I was even invited to a private luncheon for high-potential talent. This luncheon was designed to allow the senior leaders of the company an opportunity to meet those individuals who had been identified as the organization's *Rising Rock Stars.* Those who were selected and fortunate to receive this invitation were thrilled. Needless to say, I didn't sleep the night before because I was so excited. I laid out my navy blue suit, made sure I had a fresh coat of paint on my nails, practiced introducing myself in the bathroom mirror, and rehearsed my five-year career goals over and over.

During the luncheon, I met someone who I will call Ms. Cecily from the C-suite. She was the highest-ranking female executive in our company. She was the right hand to the CEO. I had only seen this woman in our company brochures and videos, so meeting her was the highlight of my afternoon. I wanted to maximize my experience for the day, so I got up the nerve to ask her to lunch, and she actually said yes!

I was assertive, ambitious, and interested in getting to the next level. However, I was naïve to inner-office politics and the role they played. What I didn't count on was Mrs. Navy Blue feeling uncomfortable about my lunch plans with Ms. Cecily from the C-Suite (which I later learned was her boss's boss). It didn't even dawn on me this would be an issue, or why.

Honestly, I thought my boss would be proud of me for taking the initiative to build this relationship. Ms. Cecily, from the C-Suite, told me I was the ONLY employee that had asked her to lunch all year!

(Go me!!!) But Mrs. Navy Blue was more curious than proud. She began asking questions like, "Why are you having lunch with her?" "Why didn't you tell me before you planned this?" "What are you going to talk about?"

My only agenda was to network at the highest levels to help my career. I had no idea later, that this would be the nail in my career coffin.

> **Fact:** A 2011 survey by the American Management Association found that 95 percent of working women polled believe they were undermined by another woman at some point in their career, while a 2008 University of Toronto study of U.S. employees found employees working under a female supervisor reported more distress and symptoms of physical stress than those working under a male supervisor.[xiv]

My lunch with Ms. Cecily from the C-Suite was great and everything I had hoped it would be. She was open, forthcoming with great career advice, and shared her personal story. I was so inspired. She even asked for my opinion on what I thought she should be doing differently. We committed to staying in touch at least once a quarter.

Looking Back: Looking back, I would have handled this situation much differently. Honestly, the proper thing to do was to inform my boss immediately after I made plans with Cecily from the C-Suite. Instead, she actually heard it from someone else. This made it appear I had something to hide. This doesn't condone her behavior, but out of respect, she should have heard it from me. If you are networking at levels above your boss's pay grade, do yourself a favor and keep them in the loop.

The Devil Appears

What I didn't know then, was things with Mrs. Navy Blue and I would never be the same. Before the famous lunch meeting with Ms.

Cecily from the C-Suite, I was a great employee, who had been invited to a private luncheon for the company's rising stars. Then overnight, everything I did, according to my boss, was wrong. There was a strong unspoken tension between us. There was silence when there used to be communication. It was clear she was either angry with me, or irritated by me. Our grab and go lunch meetings turned into email messages and sticky notes. I didn't understand what was going on.

As one of the key leaders on her team, I would often lead meetings or present on her behalf. Like clockwork, I would meet with her one week prior to the meeting to ensure we were aligned. The first team meeting post 'the lunch date' was a disaster. She berated me in front of the team, accusing me of being shortsighted and unprepared. She said that there were clear areas that I had missed, and encouraged me to do more research next time.

Please keep in mind, I met with her at least twice, before this meeting. She knew exactly what I was presenting, and even saw my talking points. I was embarrassed and humiliated. But somehow, I thought it was my fault. I thought, well, maybe I could have asked more questions. After the meeting, she called and asked me how I thought it went. She acted as if nothing happened, which created further confusion for me. Before hanging up, she casually mentioned that I should focus more on my job, instead of making lunch appointments.

The next several months, every single meeting was just like that one, except they were getting worse. I changed my strategy and started meeting with her one hour before the meeting, thinking that maybe I was actually missing something. Mrs. Navy Blue said I wasn't focused over the last few months, and appeared to be distracted (she would say this publicly in meetings). So, I literally wrote down every word I planned to say. I shared it with her. I even asked her to physically make the updates to the presentation, so I was sure I had her edits. Just like the other meetings, she would ask questions during my presentation as if she had never seen it, and shook her head in disapproval, while she took notes.

> **Fact:** A Canadian study in 2008 found that women with female supervisors had higher cases of depression, headaches, heartburn and insomnia than if their bosses were men. Little did I know, I would be part of this statistic.

Public Humiliation

Mrs. Navy Blue seemed to enjoy coaching me publicly in front of my peers. Often telling me, in a very irritated and condescending voice, that there continued to be an opportunity for me to be more prepared and strategic. She said she was disappointed and surprised because it wasn't indicative of the level of work I normally did. She lectured me and explained that not being prepared and strategic would become a barrier to my success. This was ironic because I spoke with her about wanting to apply for a promotional role that was opening soon. I didn't mind the feedback at all. I just didn't understand why she only gave it to me when she had an audience.

This continued for more than a year. There were also times when Mrs. Navy Blue would not speak to me at all. She would literally, not speak to me. If there were several people in the room and I made a comment or asked a question, she would not even acknowledge or address me. I internalized her behavior as if I had done something wrong. Becoming very insecure, I began to question my decisions and myself all of the time. I was always embarrassed.

Then one day, after another bad meeting, I received a call from one of my colleagues named Alona. Alona had been around much longer than I had, and was also a part of the private luncheon I attended. The difference was, she wasn't interested in getting promoted. She said, "Hey, are you ok?" I said, "Sure." I didn't know what she was referring to.

She said, "Mrs. Navy Blue has been beating you up all year. It's brutal, how do you take that?" I laughed it off and told her that I was fine. For some reason, I felt like I couldn't be honest about what I was feeling. Alona paused, and the silence during that phone call was so loud. She finally spoke, "Listen, just be careful. Mrs. Navy

Blue doesn't seem to have your best interest at heart. She called me today about the new role that I know you are planning to apply for. Don't worry, I am not interested, but I thought you should know. One more thing, we have been having bi-weekly team meetings without you."

Even though I knew there was an audience for this craziness over the past year, I was hoping they just didn't see it. I was embarrassed for being weak. I was humiliated. More importantly, I was pissed. I had been working my butt off to be considered for this new role that I knew was coming. I think subconsciously, I was enduring this crazy ride because I really believed I would have a serious shot at this new role. However, I would have to have the endorsement of my boss, Mrs. Navy Blue. She knew this. I couldn't even get her to talk to me about it, and my office was right next to hers. She was controlling me.

We were in weekly meetings together and each time I brought it up, she changed the subject. Most people assumed I would be the front-runner because I was pretty much doing the job already. To hear that she called my peer about the job I was preparing for, it stung.

Looking back: Looking back, I would have handled things differently. I would have sought out a mentor to discuss the things I was feeling. At the time, things felt bad, because I was so close to it. I couldn't identify that I was being bullied. But someone else could have, especially the team meetings being conducted without me. Isolation or exclusion can be indicators that there is a hostile working environment. Most companies have policies against this type of behavior, even if you don't know what to call it.

I hung up the phone, went to the parking lot, got in my car and cried. I felt so lonely. I felt like I was being bullied and pushed around, but in a passive-aggressive way. This micro-aggression was making me ill. What is micro-aggression? It is a subtle, indirect statement or discriminatory action against someone in an underrepresented group. That was me! Nothing she did by itself really rose to the occasion of committing an infraction. But everything she did felt like she was punishing me. I felt like I was being targeted. Who could I share this with?

I am one of the few African American leaders who got lucky enough to be invited to the 'private lunch'. I had a nice salary, a company car, company credit card, and a beautiful corporate office. I even had the opportunity to fly on our company's private jet. Did I really have anything to complain about? When I heard myself talk about this, it sounded like I was whining. Why would a little bit of public feedback bother me? It didn't bother me, the public humiliation was actually killing me.

I was hurting and afraid. It was like being in a fight with the wind. You can't see it, but you can feel it, and you definitely know it's there. But guess what? **CHAMPIONS NEVER TELL** and to a lot of people, I was a Champion. But in truth, I actually felt like a chump.

Fact: Thirty-five percent of Americans reported being bullied at work, according to a 2010 survey by the Workplace Bullying Institute. Women make much nastier office bullies than men, says psychologist Dr. Gary Namie, co-founder of the Institute. Workplace bullying is four times more common than sexual harassment and racial discrimination. Girls are taught to be critical about each other from adolescence, and it's particularly vicious among working women, from playing favorites to badmouthing colleagues.[xv]

Sabotage

At one point during my career, I saw going to meetings and presenting in front of senior leaders as a great opportunity. I would live for these meetings because I was a great presenter. Now, I was a nervous wreck if I knew Mrs. Navy Blue was going to be present. I would visibly shake and stutter, bracing myself for the public abrasive feedback that would always come. Sweat would pour down the back of my legs. I would soil the under arm of my shirts, and my face would turn different shades of red. I would even feel physically ill like I had to vomit. I started having migraines on a weekly basis, so I kept painkillers in my purse at all times. It was bad.

One of our big regional conferences was coming up, and I was selected by one of the divisional leaders to represent our division. People saw me as a rising star, high potential talent, and one who was next in line for big things. I was chosen to present our new division strategy and the formula that my boss created. This formula was complicated. I scheduled a meeting with her to get a few key talking points. I wanted to review the formula, the calculations (because I am not that great with numbers) and suggestions for presentation delivery.

To my surprise, she was extremely helpful and offered to make the handouts for the meeting. This felt like the best interaction we had in a very long time. Her tone was soft and caring. She checked in with me to see how I was feeling right before the presentation. She talked about how this exposure would be good for me. I started to feel like maybe things weren't so bad after all. Maybe it was just me not being as prepared as I should have been, and she was really in my corner.

My presentation started off strong. I was nervous because she was present, and her ability to be critical in a public setting still sent chills up my spine. I was also nervous because I hated numbers, figures, and statistics, and I had to present all three. Vomiting before presentations had become the norm. Halfway through my presentation, I looked around the room and noticed that people were flipping through the pages, appearing to be lost. They had these confusing looks on their faces. I stopped the presentation and directed them to the correct page number. Guess what? They had the wrong presentation.

I looked at my boss and she said she must have printed the wrong file. She encouraged me to continue, and present from the screen. I moved forward, however, the excel spreadsheet was difficult to see from the screen, which is why the handouts were so important. This created a need for the leaders in the room to ask more questions than usual, which I was dreading. They even asked if I could just start the presentation over because they weren't following me.

This would have been the perfect time for Mrs. Navy Blue to jump in and offer some assistance since she was the creator of the formula and had distributed the wrong presentation. Silence. Nothing. The room became quiet and awkward. It took everything in me not to run out of there. My boss finally said, "We'll provide an update in our next meeting when Jil is a bit more prepared. I will help her. My apologies team."

I just stood there, while she explained my lack of preparation and how I was still growing. I even thought I saw her smirk in my direction. This was sabotage. In the room was the Division President, and members of the senior leadership team. Keep in mind, I inquired about applying for a role that to would be considered a promotion.

These moments of public humiliation began to take its toll on me. My heart was always racing, the migraines were getting worse, and it became difficult for me to concentrate. She went from humiliating me publicly to calling me on my cell phone at 8 and 9 pm at night. It was always for a reason that could wait until morning, but this was her way of saying, "I am the boss."

Facts: In a Workplace Bullying Institute online survey, *The Toll of Workplace Bullying on Employee Health,* 71 percent of the 516 respondents reported having been treated by a doctor for work-related health symptoms; 63 percent reported seeing a mental health professional. Of the top health-related symptoms, many included physical as well as mental health-related issues, including:

- High Blood Pressure
- Migraine Tension Headaches
- Heart Palpitations/Anxiety
- Loss of Concentration/Memory
- Mood Swings/ Tremors
- Irritable Bowel Syndrome

I had transformed from a strong, ambitious and confident rising young professional, to a very insecure person. I literally felt incompetent. I used to be a strong public speaker that was confident and enthusiastic. I began to stutter, stumble and literally shake from being nervous. At this point, I hadn't told anyone. I was embarrassed and didn't want anyone to know. Heck, I didn't know what to say. Would I tell them Mrs. Navy Blue gives me negative feedback publicly? Or that she doesn't speak to me. Or that she printed the wrong file. Those don't sound like awful things and definitely not worth reporting. These are all things I should be able to handle... right?

People admired me because they thought I was strong, and I didn't want them to see the truth. The truth was, I cried. A lot. At night. On the way to work, and on the way home from work. I felt alone and weak. I thought I was the only one, so I suffered in silence. I told no one.

Looking back: *Looking back, I would have handled things differently. I would have gone to the doctor had my symptoms checked out. The truth is, I have always had a few stomach problems, but due to my consistent nervous nature, I had diarrhea all of the time. I had all of the physical, mental and emotional symptoms that said I was headed for a nervous breakdown. I should have gone to the doctor. Today, most companies have an EAP (Employee Assistance Program) available. It's a confidential service, and often times, you get up to three free sessions.*

More than Just a Bad Boss!

I didn't get the promotion I applied for, which meant I had to stay in the living hell with her. I look back on my experience and I ask myself why didn't I say more? Why didn't I report this? The honest answer is that I simply didn't have a name for it. Sexual harassment or racial discrimination are often times, easily identifiable behaviors for most people. But, I couldn't identify what was happening to me at the time. I felt that I had a bad boss but what

Champion can't handle that? As I look back, this was more than just having a bad boss.

The silent treatment, constant public humiliation, intimidation, lack of support, being ostracized from meetings, are all indicators of an unhealthy environment, and in this case, workplace bullying and a hostile working environment. It all started after I had contact with her superior. I didn't have a name for what was happening at the time, but I did know it wasn't right, because **CHAMPIONS NEVER TELL**.

Fact: Only a quarter to a third of people who have been harassed at work report it to a supervisor or union representative, and two percent to 13 percent file a formal complaint. Mostly, they fear retaliation, and with good reason, research shows.

Some don't report a problem because they don't think their experience qualifies as illegal harassment. Many victims, who are most often women, fear they will face disbelief, inaction, blame or societal and professional retaliation. That could be hostility from supervisors, a bad reference to future employers, or the loss of job opportunities. A study of public-sector employees, two-thirds of workers, who complained about mistreatment, described some form of retaliation in a follow-up survey.[xvi]

Looking Back: As I look back, I would have handled these situations differently. I would have paid more attention to what I was feeling. I would have been journaling my incidents of discomfort, and I would have talked to someone who could help change the environment I was in. I would also have made a decision to leave sooner, once I realized I was being devalued. Remember, you work there because you want to. You are valuable, and your talent will be appreciated elsewhere. I just didn't have the managerial courage at the time. Don't let that be you!

STORM #2

Nice Ass!

Every year, our division goes away for two days to conduct our off-site retreat. The company's senior leaders often attended to build relationships with those of us they don't know and to contribute to helping us build our plan. Our team looked forward to these off sites because my boss did a great job with dividing up our time between fun team building activities and our strategy meetings. He was great at doing this.

One of our senior leaders arrived to the retreat early this year. I'll call him 'Mr. Navy Blue Blazer.' It seemed like he always had on a navy blue blazer, with a light powder blue button-down shirt underneath, and no tie. He was a white male, about 6"4, had blond hair and was a bit intimidating. He wore light brown khakis with navy blue leather casual loafers. He and my boss were scheduled to meet, and one of my male colleagues and I were invited to join. Every now and then, my boss would invite some of the leaders on his team to meetings that he thought would be good for our exposure and development.

As I entered the room, I noticed that my male colleague, my boss, and Mr. Navy Blue Blazer were already talking. This is commonly known as, 'The Meeting before the Meeting.' This is where the real decisions are made. Mr. Navy Blue Blazer put down his pen, took off his glasses and said, "Ah, yes! I was hoping someone was bringing coffee."

My boss looked up embarrassed and said, "No, Jil is also part of my team. She will be joining us for the meeting. I can get coffee brought in if you like." Mr. Navy Blue paused, put his glasses back on and said, "Oh, sorry. Well Doll, can you take notes for us?"

The meeting lasted about an hour. During the meeting, my boss's admin, Gina, arrived with coffee and a few refreshments for us to eat while we met. The small group decided they would go play a quick round of golf before the rest of the team arrived. Honestly, I was sitting there a little nervous about playing golf because I wasn't that good. But I told myself that would go anyway.

Right in the middle of my thought, Mr. Navy Blue Blazer turned to me and said, "Hey Honey, can you clean this up while we go get ready to play a round? You people do great at this kind of stuff."

Silence. I said, "You People?"

He said, "You know, the support team people."

There was an awkward silence. My boss looked at me and shrugged and said, "Do you mind? Gina has left for the day." Before I could answer, all three of them walked out. I stood there fuming. Not only was I the only woman, but I was also the only person of color in the room. Mr. Navy Blue Blazer assumed that I was the coffee lady (not that I am opposed to bringing anyone coffee), not someone attending the meeting.

He then referred to me as 'Doll' and asked me to take notes (again, I don't have a problem with taking notes), and then, I was asked to clean up!! What century are we living in?! Not to mention, during the entire meeting, Mr. Navy Blue Blazer only addressed my male colleague with conversation. It was bizarre. The one time he did speak in my direction he said, "Doll, are you able to keep up with this?"

__Looking back:__ I would have handled this differently. I would have attempted to find another resource to support the cleaning initiative. For example, I could have said, "Hey, let me grab a couple of folks to help us out with this, so we all can go." At that point, they would have been forced to tell me no. They would have had to say out loud, we don't want you.

At the end of our retreat, we had the infamous company luau. Everyone had a lei around their neck, the island music was loud, and the food smelled amazing. This was an incredible way to end a couple days of long meetings. I was headed to the drink station to grab some wine when I saw Mr. Navy Blue Blazer walking toward my direction. He nodded as he passed by me, then I felt someone grab my butt. I stopped, turned around and he said, "Nice ass!" with a smirk that looked like The Joker from Batman. I was mortified, speechless, embarrassed and felt violated.

I was sick to my stomach the next day when my office line rang and it was him. He said he was following up personally with all of the junior leaders to see how we enjoyed the retreat. He wanted to make sure we thought the time spent was value added…and then laughed. Later that week, I was in a one on one with my boss. As we wrapped up our time together, I asked him if I could share something with him. My boss was, for the most part, supportive and pretty understanding.

He said sure. I began to tell him that Mr. Navy Blue Blazer made me feel uncomfortable. He began to chuckle, and said, "Yeah, he told me you guys had a bit of a run in."

I said, "What run in? He touched me."

He said, "He mentioned he literally bumped into you when getting wine, and that you looked startled." My face must have said everything, because I never said a word. My boss said, "Are you ok?"

I said, "No."

He said, "Well, I am glad you are not one of those whining women who make a big deal out of small things. That normally doesn't end well."

Thirty days later, our company went through a major restructuring. My boss was moved to a different state on a new assignment, and Mr. Navy Blue Blazer became our new boss. In our first team meeting, he turned to me and said, "It's so refreshing to see that you are actually pretty and bright. Tomorrow, I would like for you to ride with me as I tour this new market and meet the managers." He smiled, and I almost threw up.

Facts: Roughly 70% of those who experience sexual harassment at work don't tell a superior about it, according to a report from the EEOC. They did not report harassment against themselves or others because of fear of retaliation by the harasser or organization.

Looking back: Looking back, I would have handled this differently. I would have immediately shared the 'nice ass' tap to my boss. I then would have immediately filed a complaint with the Human Resource Dept. It shouldn't matter that there were no witnesses. It happened to me, so therefore, I should have told. Because had it happened again, it would have been on file and he would be held accountable. By me speaking up, it would give him the message that he couldn't treat me that way. My silence almost appeared like it gave him permission. Remember, most companies have strict policies against sexual harassment. Don't wait for it to happen more than once, report this behavior right away.

STORM #3

A Slap in the Face

I was sitting at my oversized mahogany desk, staring out the window. I needed to look away from the computer screen because my eyes were getting tired. There was a light knock on my door. I looked up and saw someone I will call, 'Navy Blue Bags' standing in my doorway.

She was a short, petite young African-American woman, who wore a short, jet-black bob, with light brown highlights that complimented her smooth brown complexion that looked like she had been kissed by the sun. She had been with the company for about two years, and she always carried a navy blue oversized Louis Vuitton purse. I learned later, this was a gift from her fiancé. Our meeting had been scheduled for a couple of weeks, but I had honestly forgotten.

She asked me to be her mentor, and I immediately said yes. I believe in the power of mentorship and I believe every woman should not only have one, but should be one as well. Studies show that women who have mentors excel at a faster pace than those who don't. Navy Blue Bags was ambitious and wanted to be promoted that year. She was brilliant, a graduate of Cornell University, and was in the process of completing her MBA degree.

We discussed the role she wanted and the areas she felt like she needed to strengthen. She mentioned that she really wanted help with her executive presence. She said she admired the way that I dressed, my makeup and even how I styled my hair. I told her that I would be thrilled to help her with executive presence, but the first thing we would do is to get a 360 leadership survey completed. This is a survey that an employee will send out to selected direct reports, peers and their leadership. The selected individuals give feedback on the employee's strengths and areas that need to be developed.

While we waited for the results to come back, I suggested we go shopping since she mentioned she wanted to change up her look. This was one of the worst things I could have ever done. Our first stop was a popular designer makeup counter. We got her makeup done and experimented with new shades of foundation, eye shadow and lipstick. The expression on her face was of disappointment after she saw how much the makeup cost. After all of that, she wasn't going to be able to purchase any of it. So, when she walked away, I discreetly handed my credit card to the sales rep and surprised her with the makeup later. She was thrilled. Honestly, this wasn't good judgment. I should not have done this.

We began to spend more time together and develop a pretty good relationship. The 360 survey results finally came back. I was shocked. They were terrible. The feedback was consistent from her direct reports, her coworkers, and her direct supervisor. She was rude, intimidating, difficult to work with, and lacked integrity. As a matter of fact, one of the accusations made against her resulted in an investigation the year before.

Mean Girl

I'd heard a few rumblings here and there, but the details never reached my level until then. When I sat with her to give her the feedback, she became defensive and curt. She accused the organization of being racist and trying to sabotage her career. Her voice began to elevate and she became unprofessional. She started using profanity and stated if she wasn't an "N" she would be promoted by now. She said, "I am sure you know what I mean?" I firmly told her that her behavior was out of line and unprofessional, and that I wouldn't tolerate her speaking this way to me.

I have to admit, I was pretty surprised. This wasn't reflective of my interaction prior to this moment. However, it supported the feedback that I had just read. She asked if she could be excused and quickly left my office. That moment changed everything. As I was driving home that night, she called my cell phone and apologized. She said she was under a lot of pressure, and wanted to know if she could come over my house to finish talking.

I told her I thought that was inappropriate and not a good idea. She then insisted we meet for coffee the next morning. I told her I was unavailable and ended the conversation. The following months were very strange. She stopped showing up for our mentoring appointments, for which I was grateful, and she had become distant. Then, I got a call one day from the Human Resources Department informing me that she had applied for a promotional role and listed me as her mentor. They asked for feedback.

I hadn't seen her for months since the outburst in my office, except for one Sunday when I saw her at my church. This had to be a coincidence. It was weird and when I went over to say hi, she wouldn't speak. I then saw her at the grocery store near my neighborhood while I was there shopping with my kids. She was alone, walked past me with her cart, and still didn't speak. Another time, I swear it seemed like I spotted her car parked next to mine at the movie theater. Something weird was happening.

The next day at work, I had a flat tire. There was a large construction nail sticking out of the side. The roadside assistance guy informed me that the location of the nail didn't reflect that I had rolled over something. It almost appeared as if someone put it there intentionally.

Honestly, I had become a little nervous and uneasy. My gut was telling me that something was going on, but I didn't know what. I recall walking into one of the employee break rooms and literally, all the conversations stopped.

Then one day, a team member stopped me in the hallway and said, "What happened between you and Navy Blue Bags?" I looked puzzled and said, "What do you mean?" She told me that Navy Blue Bags was telling other employees that she hated me and that I was bullying her and blocking her from being promoted. I blew this off because it sounded ridiculous.

Me? Bullying her? With all the help I had given this young lady? She was feeling insecure about her makeup and I bought her the new makeup that she picked out. When I learned that she was struggling financially, I had a few people come together to give her a gift card that would help her to buy food, and a few household items. When I found out her dad passed away and she couldn't afford to fly home, I stayed with her for hours on the phone researching flights until we found an affordable one. When she wanted to apply for the promotion, I helped her prepare for the interview. When she wanted to meet certain leaders, I arranged the meetings. When her fiancé married someone else, I sent her flowers. I knew there had to be a misunderstanding. However, something was up, and I would find out very soon.

Betrayal

The next day, I received a call from my boss. He informed me that a complaint had been filed against me. I couldn't for the life of me, figure out what it could be about, or whom it could be from. This person called our corporate Human Resources Department, so I was horrified. Because this was raised as a concern, the corporate Human Resources Department had to conduct the investigation. I was embarrassed and confused. My reputation and possibly my job, were on the line.

I read the complaint and discovered that it was Navy Blue Bags that filed it! She complained that I was harassing her, and blocking her from promotional opportunities! In the report, there was a copy of the makeup receipt from the purchase I made for her, dates we met for our mentor sessions, the people that she shared her concerns with, the job description for the role she applied for, and a doctor's note stating that she was suffering from workplace stress.

The complaint said that I bullied her because I didn't like the way that she looked and criticized her publicly. It also stated that I stalked her, pressured her to meet with me, and forced her to change her makeup. She further stated in the complaint that I told her if she wanted to get promoted, she had to look more like me. She said what really made her uncomfortable is when I tried to get her to spend the night at my house. This was ridiculous. Was this real?

The words to describe how I felt, were numb, shocked, and betrayed. I felt as though someone had punched me in the stomach. This was a young lady who asked **me** to become her mentor. I felt inclined to make myself available as a resource because she was a woman and a woman who was African-American like me.

Later, I found out she was trying to get a petition signed by other employees to get me fired! How did I find this out? I had a great relationship with our custodial staff. They were my favorite department. They were mostly men and women my grandparents' age that adored me just as much as I adored them. One in particular, who I will call 'Ms. Fire Cracker', always brought me homemade soup or bread to work when she prepared it for her family.

One evening, Ms. Fire Cracker and one of her coworkers were waiting by my car in the parking garage. She had a serious look on her face. She said, "Sweetheart, I have to tell you something. I was cleaning the boardroom the other night when a few employees asked if they could use the room for a quick meeting. I kept cleaning while they met. They were talking about getting other employees to sign some paper that said you are a bad leader. The goal is to get you fired." I said, "What!? Are you sure?" She said she didn't know their names but described the one who was leading the charge. Guess who? Yep. It was Navy Blue Bags. This was a slap in the face.

The investigation into the complaint lasted about two weeks. It felt like forever. The findings of the investigation didn't support her allegations. They even interviewed the few people who signed the petition, and they all eventually admitted they were just going along with it for a free dinner she promised them.

I was relieved the investigation was over, but needless to say, I was very disappointed. I was disappointed that another woman that I had tried so hard to help was working so hard against me. I was hurt and devastated that another woman was literally trying to destroy my career. I was embarrassed for women. I was embarrassed for African-American women. I was disappointed that she blamed me for her missed career opportunities, instead of owning the feedback for herself. This could have turned out differently if I didn't have such a strong reputation already with people from different levels of the organization who spoke up on my behalf.

When asked why she was trying to get me fired, she said that "I wasn't looking out for other sistas."

Looking back: Looking back, I would have handled things differently. First of all, I would have kept my interaction with her strictly professional. I actually got too personally involved. The lack of boundaries is what created the expectations. I would have also waited (like I normally did) for the 360 results to come back, to understand more about the mentee's strengths and areas of opportunity. Once she became disrespectful and unprofessional in the meeting that day, I should have addressed this through the proper channels. I felt like she was stalking me but I couldn't prove it. I should have brought this to the attention of my leadership because once she filed a complaint against me, she had receipts and other documentation and I had nothing. Unfortunately, I didn't think I needed that. I was so focused on helping a young woman and being a mentor. I still believe in mentorship today. I am just much more responsible.

Summary

Storm #1: Mrs. Navy Blue

Micro aggression, Hostile Working Environment, Bullying and Sabotage

Mrs. Navy Blue was a strong professional female role model that I hoped to learn and grow from. I automatically assumed that I would find a mentor, advocate, and career champion in her. But what I found was a woman who was insecure, who created a hostile working environment. Her micro aggressions caused me to become stressed and physically ill. This kind of harassment and sabotage is more frequent than you would believe. I didn't identify as one being bullied. According to studies, this form of harassment happens more than sexual harassment and racial discrimination.

Storm #2: Mr. Navy Blue Blazer

Invisible Syndrome, Sexual Harassment, Intimidation

Mr. Navy Blue was a high achieving, highly educated white male professional who struggled with diversity and inclusion. He had a hard time believing that women or women of color could contribute outside of service/servant roles. He believed that there were no boundaries or consequences for his actions. I was invisible in meetings and frequently regulated to the note taker. I didn't have support from leadership, and my silence probably empowered his poor behavior. Worse, he eventually became my boss.

Storm #3: Navy Blue Bag

Intimidation, Sabotage

Navy Blue Bags was a young African American professional looking for mentorship, guidance, and support. Our relationship turned toxic when she started to plot against, undermine and attempt to sabotage my career. Ms. Navy Blue Bags became extremely vindictive and tried to intimidate me through stalking. She also attempted to turn others against me. This is an example of what we hear often of women not supporting each other. We know that this behavior is not the standard, but we should be aware that it happens.

These are several examples of working in a hostile environment where I was being bullied and didn't realize it. This is happening around the world every day. Studies show women are bullied more often than men and don't tell. Not weak women. **Winning Women**. There is a misconception that strong, high achieving women can't get bullied, or mistreated. The reality is, it can happen to anybody. This experience made me stronger. I offer the steps below as I took ownership of my outcomes.

My Advice For You...

1. Center yourself. Spend the first 30 minutes of your day in quiet time. I read the Bible and pray. This centers me and gives me the strength I need to face whatever the day brings.

2. Build your mental mettle. Every morning, I read or listen to something that helps me develop a healthy mindset. It might be Tony Robbins, Iyanla Vanzant, or Brene' Brown, etc.

3. Know your stuff. Study the policies and procedures at work. Know what your rights are and what the process is if you have to share a concern. This is important and empowers you to act on your own behalf. This will also help you identify if something inappropriate is happening to you.

4. Use your voice. The best person to speak up for you is you. This is where I failed myself before, but not anymore. A real champion advocates for themselves and sometimes, that does include telling.

5. Get a mentor. Find a mentor and meet with them at least once a month. If I had a mentor at the time, I could have shared my concerns and challenges. Instead, I was isolated and no one knew what was happening. A mentor can also be instrumental in becoming an advocate for you as well.

6. Rock your career plan. Map out your own year career plan. You don't have to wait on HR. It's your life! Let's go! Join a broader group. Isolation is the enemy of anyone who wants to progress their career. Join a professional organization that supports your industry, become a star, and leverage the resources offered.

Be extra: Volunteer for extra assignments or projects that will bring you additional development and visibility. This will go a long way. You are now building a base of supporters and advocates that are outside of just your immediate supervisor. This way, your entire career isn't just built on your interaction with a Mrs. Navy Blue.

Facts: Workplace bullying takes place in very many different contexts and forms. Workplace bullying is a pattern of hostile messages and abusive behaviors persistently targeted at one or more persons in work settings that can involve work obstruction, public humiliation, verbal abuse, threatening behavior, and multiple forms of intimidation. Amongst others, workplace bullying is characterized by repetition (occurs regularly), duration(endures), escalation (increasing aggression), power disparity (the target lacks the power to successfully defend themselves), and attributed intent. Repetition - Workplace bullying is mostly a repeated behavior, though there are some singular events. It often involves numerous hostile interactions and transactions (e.g. verbal abuse and public humiliation coupled with social ostracism, work obstruction, and destructive gossip). Duration - Again, workplace bullying occurs frequently and extends over long periods of time. Persistence makes bullying particularly harmful and corrosive, wearing down the targets' defenses, social support, and health. Escalation - Adams and Crawford (1992)

Chapter 3

LIFE BEAT THE LIFE OUT OF ME
By Christy Rutherford

"What is success? It is being able to go to bed each night with
your soul at peace." ~Paulo Coelho

Five years ago, I was tired. Tired of fighting for respect. Tired of
fighting the men in my male-dominated work environment. Tired
from fighting the women who didn't understand my drive. Tired of
giving all of my energy to everyone else and not reserving any for
myself.

Most of all, I was EXHAUSTED from fighting with myself and
the voice in my head. I was tired of MYSELF. I no longer
recognized the person staring back at me in the mirror and frankly, I
didn't like her.

Although I was highly successful, considered a great leader and
mentored a lot of people, I weaved a web around myself that was
choking me out. I felt like I was drowning on dry land. When you're
everyone else's hero, no one checks on you. You can't show your
weaknesses or say that you're tired. You continue to give and give
and give, even when you have nothing left.

As a leader, I had to show up every day ready to serve, but
something had to change, or I was going to die. After a series of
events, including a "cray cray boss," I burned out and resigned from
a successful six-figure career, and ran away from everything and
everyone I knew with 3.5 years left to retire with a full pension.

It was remnant of the movie scene when Tina Turner (played by
Angela Bassett) fled for her life and ran down the street hysterically,
in a white suit after she finally decided to leave her abusive husband.
She arrived at a hotel, battered and bruised, and didn't have anything
but her name and her talent.

Feeling like I'd been abused enough, I didn't know what was on the other side of darkness, but knew everything would be okay because of my skills and talents. Life had beat the life out of me and after getting to a safe place, I asked myself,

"How did this happen?"

"How did you allow yourself to get to this place of absolute depletion before you took action?!!"

"Why did you stay so long?"

"How did you get here, and how are you going to get all of your marbles back?"

Oh yeah.... I was missing a few marbles. LOL! If we were gifted 100 marbles at birth, and give them up along the journey of life, I only had two left and they were at the risk of turning into dust.

Unaware of my value in the market, I was offered four jobs the first week after resigning, 10 in the first two months, and over 30 within three years. I kept job offers for entertainment purposes because I didn't want to work for anyone. I was no longer looking for money, prestige, awards, material possessions or success... I had those already. I wanted my marbles back!!

How could I be so full professionally, and so empty personally? I felt like a hollow Easter Bunny...dressed in a shiny gold foil wrapper and red bow. But if you had peeled one layer back and bitten off my ear, there wouldn't have been anything on the inside. I'd given away all I could give in the quest for success, and felt there was nothing left to give.

After taking some time to examine this predicament, I realized I had A LOT of work to do!! One of my favorite quotes from Napoleon Hill is....

"If...I had the courage to see myself as I really am, I would find out what is wrong with me, and correct it, then I might have a chance to profit by my mistakes and learn something from the experience of others, for I know that there is something WRONG with me, or I would now be where I WOULD HAVE BEEN IF I had spent more time analyzing my weaknesses, and less time building alibis to cover them."

Ahhhh..... Looking in the mirror. Being self-reflective and taking 100 percent responsibility for every single result that I had in my life. I was responsible for the good and the bad, but taking responsibility for the bad was startling and excruciating. However, I knew that in order to create real change in my life, I had to start with the woman in the mirror.

Hitting The Reset Button

Over the past five years, I've invested thousands of hours in personal development, which included reading hundreds of books, repeatedly listening to audiobooks, watching videos of some of the world's greatest leaders, and investing over six figures at events, camps, and training.

I chose to work on MYSELF just as hard as I worked on my career. I needed to get back to my center. I didn't know what I would find or where I left my marbles, but I knew I'd recognize them when I found them.

Walking in darkness, and being guided by a higher power, I had to feel my way back to wholeness, inner peace, and joy. I traced a line and connected the dots on most of the actions I took to become successful. That was fun. I also connected the dots on how I ended up unhealthy, stressed, single, and self-conscious. Albeit difficult, there were some gems found, and once the unknown was known, there was a chance to break the cycle and create a new reality.

For the most part, I hit the reset button and started my life over again. At a certain point, I stopped looking backward while trying to fix a broken past, and just surrendered fully to creating a new life. It's taken a loooooong time and A LOT of work to stand in who I AM authentically and unapologetically.

With great success, I finally retrieved my missing marbles and realized money couldn't buy any of them. In fact, we are given these marbles free of charge at birth, but surrender them for money and high levels of success. The marbles were self-love, joy, happiness, unconditional love for others, inner peace, perfect health, a restored connection with family, patience, and an open mind towards people....among other things.

Looking Back

I loved my previous organization. I loved our mission, the people who worked for me as well as those I served with. The insight I'm sharing here is not intended to demean an organization where I have lifelong friends or the people that I consider to be family. I would like to highlight that constantly justifying this is exactly why women suffer silently, because we're concerned about dishonoring others and the brands of the organizations to our detriment.

During my career, I rarely saw a large number of women leaders in high-ranking positions. It was hardly ever a topic of discussion, but an eye sore for other women. When people want to be inspired, they look for people who look like them for inspiration. If there isn't anyone who looks similar by race/ethnicity, there are going to be challenges. The lack of gender similarities only compounds the issue.

Recruited in a program to increase minority representation, I was one of nearly 50 black women officers in my organization. Fifty women of nearly 300 black officers out of 47,000 people made black women officers 0.1 percent of the organization and black officers 0.6 percent.

I often wondered why we didn't have a larger number of black leaders in the higher ranks, but when you only have a dismal number of leaders to start with, there isn't much opportunity to create a pipeline of people to be represented in large numbers at high levels.

Year after year, I listened as senior leaders told conference rooms full of people that black women, and women in general, were falling short. They said we left the organization at critical points in our careers to start families. This was a consistent explanation that easily rolled off of their tongues, but there was no basis for it, and no studies to back it up.

Over my career, I met a number of women who had the talent, abilities, and grit to make it to the higher levels, but somehow, fell short. I didn't understand their obstacles and hindrances, until I was promoted several times and started to see the challenges first hand.

Since the number of minorities overall were pretty low, when we walked in a room, we instantly stood out. There were incidents that occurred over my career that had become normal, but looking back, I was in a toxic and hostile work environment every single day, but didn't realize it.

For example, as minorities, we weren't allowed to sit beside each other and talk to each other. It would make the majority members nervous, so in order to keep the peace, we avoided conversation or hanging out with each other while at work. We used to laugh it off as a joke if we talked to each other longer than 10 minutes. People would pass us and slow down to let us know that they "noticed." If it was more than two minorities....WHOA! We normalized what wasn't funny or normal.

Of the 18 supervisors I had, three of them made my life very challenging. There would be one bad year followed by three good ones. One terrible year, followed by two great ones. The good thing about being in the military is that we rotate every two to three years.

Depending on the timing, someone had to leave, so a bad boss could be waited out or we would count down the clock to our departure.

In addition to the three tyrants that I had, there were also the weekly/monthly subtle and obvious forms of disrespect. At the entry source (boot camp) and officer school, common themes were expressed to me and the other minorities.

"Why are you here?"

"You don't belong here."

"You'll never be good enough."

Can't forget their favorite... "You only got here because of Affirmative Action."

It became my mission to prove them wrong. I committed to being better, to work harder, and to shine brighter. As time continued to pass, there were additional naysayers, and it became a never-ending cycle of working endlessly to prove everyone wrong.

I got caught up in the battle for respect and acceptance, and lost sight of what was important. The quest for high levels of success while fighting to be seen and accepted came at a high cost.

Feeling Invisible Early In My Career

After spending the first two years of my career chasing drug runners in the Caribbean, I got an office job. The previous job felt never ending, and the life-threatening work was exhausting. We had a great crew and I built a solid reputation and credibility with those I served with. Although I had challenges on the ship, things were good. I wanted an EASY office job, but that proved to be very different than I imagined.

A few weeks into my new job, I was stunned that some of the junior white men in the office were very disrespectful. They would move swiftly past me in the hallway, almost knocking me down and wouldn't say excuse me. In the military, the junior people are REQUIRED to move out of the way of the senior person, but apparently, that didn't apply to me.

Coming from a ship with narrow hallways, the practice was more common and noticeable. This was the foundational experience of my career to measure the different treatment and expectations.

The junior personnel were outwardly disrespectful with physical aggression and not just the disparaging looks that I'd grown accustomed to by being one of the few black female officers in the organization. Frustrated, I confronted their supervisors and explained that the junior personnel didn't have to move out of my way completely, but I didn't want to be pushed out of the way.

One of them said, "These guys are good workers. Just leave them alone."

I was infuriated because these leaders allowed these young guys to be disrespectful, while still considering them good workers. Over the next few months, not only were some of the junior members disrespectful, they knew that their supervisors supported it, so this increased the number that did it. To get away with disrespecting a senior person was enticing to them, so several more joined in the fun.

This caused a tug of war and power struggle between me and some of my colleagues. My coworkers and friends were mostly white men, and they didn't understand why I was making such a "big deal" out of something that seemed minute to them. They never witnessed it and weren't being harassed or disrespected, so they didn't know how I felt.

The physical aggression grew, and I was being taunted and harassed every single day for months. Since their leaders declined to do their jobs, one day in frustration, I told one of the junior people, "Don't knock me down!" He went and told his supervisors, and they got mad and told me not to ever talk to him like that again.

Although I was being victimized, I was not a victim for long. After six months, one day, I snapped and decided to take matters into my own hands. I went on a tirade and threatened physical harm to the supervisors and the junior people if one of them ever disrespected me again. I became a tornado of energy, and after that day, they didn't harass me again.

This created a whole set of issues when it came to how I was seen as a young leader. It was a double-edged sword. When I didn't say anything, I was perceived as weak. When I set it off, I was perceived as a bully and too sensitive. Whether internalizing the disrespect or reacting to it, I suffered from both.

In frustration and utter disgust for what was going on, I wanted to resign and leave my job, but the rage from being disrespected, laughed at and considered weak, erupted my body in disease. I developed stress-induced arthritis, and the medication was nearly $8,000 a month. Since I had 100 percent medical coverage, I felt like I was better off staying to keep the health benefits, dismissing the fact that the hostile environment was creating the health problems. I was 25 years old.

Unable to walk long distances, I had handicap sign for six months. After a year of suffering, crying nightly and blaming others for my disease, nothing changed. In a moment of despair, I made up in my mind that being crippled was not my destiny.

I realized that rage and anger had consumed me, and played a major role in the disease. Within a few months of managing my anger and eliminating potatoes, I put my arthritis into remission and stopped taking medication altogether.

"Anxiety quickly demoralizes the whole body, and lays it open to the entrance of disease; while impure thoughts, even if not physically indulged, will sooner shatter the nervous system."
– James Allen

Mind Games and Emotional Manipulation

A year later, my direct supervisor started harassing me by talking down to me and blaming me for stuff that wasn't my job. He said he was disappointed in my work, but the work he spoke of didn't even belong in our department. After a few months of being harassed daily, my nerves became so bad that I started shaking. My health started deteriorating again, and my self-esteem was in the dumps. I couldn't sleep and wasn't eating well. The stress from it all was crushing.

Because of this, I became careless and left a safe open that contained classified material. Summoned into his office, I sat there shaking and in complete shame. As I looked down at the floor, he asked begrudgingly, "Christy, what happened here? How could you be so careless??"

I said, "Sir, I'm sorry. I've been losing sleep over the evaluation numbers you showed me a few weeks ago. I always thought if I worked hard for you, that I wouldn't have to worry about my evaluations. I don't know how I got so far off track that you would give me low numbers and it has stressed me out so bad, that I had an error in judgment and left the safe open."

He slumped in his chair. Now feeling bad, he said in a low tone, "Oh...you thought I was serious? I didn't mean that... Christy, you're a great performer, but you're such a non-emotional person. I was just trying to get a rise out of you. And since you never reacted, I was going to keep trying until you did."

I straightened up in my chair and looked at him like I was going to burn a hole through his forehead. In complete disbelief, I said, "Sir, I have been trained by my previous leaders to follow direction and do what I'm told WITHOUT question or reaction. You will NEVER get a rise out of me or see me cry in front of you. It's unprofessional and uncalled for. I have been working nearly 90 hours a week and you're harassing me because you want to get a rise out of me? You're playing games to test my emotions, instead of seeing my commitment?"

My career was jeopardized because I allowed someone to manipulate my emotions through the fear of not being promoted, and I promised to never allow a supervisor to affect me like that again.

The Last Straw

With 16 years into a highly successful career that I planned to span past 25 years, after a year of high performance in another office, a tyrant from a previous office became my supervisor again.

The harassment was swift and widespread. He harassed everyone, and I was on a mission to stop him from creating a toxic work culture, similar to the one he created five years earlier. He had a reputation in the organization for being a tyrant, so I called leaders outside of the office and asked them for advice on how to mitigate his toxicity into our culture that had become a highly productive and harmonious one.

When I sought counsel from my mentors and higher level leaders, they told me to file a Civil Rights Complaint. However, it didn't fit the legal description because he wasn't harassing me because I was black and/or a woman. He harassed EVERYONE!

Junior and senior white men were exposed to his toxicity at the same level as a senior black woman, so it wasn't a Civil Rights' issue. It was a leadership issue! I wanted someone in leadership to handle a toxic leader and not just expect for me "use my legal rights as a black woman" to file a complaint in a system that didn't work.

Either way, my career was on the line. If I didn't do something, he was going to stop me from being promoted. If I did something, I ran the risk of being retaliated against and wouldn't be promoted. I figured if I was going to go down, I would go down fighting for myself and the people that I was responsible for leading. They may have seen other leaders fail us, but they wouldn't see that I failed them. I used every channel available to stop him.

After a few months, my arthritis that was in remission for 12 years came back. From all the stress, my immune system was shot and I went to the emergency room several times a month with flu-like symptoms. I woke up and went to bed with blinding headaches that lasted all day. I had chronic back pain, and gumball sized knots in my shoulders, neck, and back. My ears started ringing, and I had secret panic attacks at my desk.

"Instead of asking what's the matter with you, you should ask WHO's the matter with you... Unforgiveness is the most prolific cause of disease." - Florence Scovel Shinn

Eventually, he found out that I had been talking to leaders outside of the office, and sent word through the #2 leader that he planned to destroy me. I asked the #2 leader what he planned to do about it, since he was being harassed too. I also asked how he could let him do that to me after all I'd done for the office, and HIM! He put his head down and said that he couldn't help me.

After a series of events, I ended up resigning with 3.5 years left to retire. Learning how volatile my career was from the previous office, I'd saved nearly six-figures. I created a break in case of emergency fund, also known as "go to h*ll money" so I bet all my chips on black and jumped off a cliff into the darkness, knowing that I'd be okay.

To leave with such a short time left to retire, I was harshly criticized and ridiculed by the people who were close to me, but they didn't know the extent of my suffering. They called me a quitter and thought that one person ran me out of my job, but they didn't know I had been harassed for most of my career. They never knew, because **CHAMPIONS NEVER TELL**

I burned out and left the organization broken and bitter. I carried immense shame for allowing my health to deteriorate that badly. I was diagnosed with PTSD and had over 15 medical conditions. Only two people knew that.

After you leave the military, the government compensates you for your medical conditions/injuries that were attained during your time in service, but I never turned in the paperwork. I didn't want to accept the money, because if I accepted the money, that means that *I BELIEVED* what they said about me was true and *THAT WAS A LIE*!! This was completely unorthodox, but I didn't want to accept a permanent diagnosis for something I considered to be temporary.

Napoleon Hill said, "I have the power to control and direct my own mind into whatever means I desire." I'll say it again, "I have the power to control and direct my own mind into whatever means I desire."

After conquering arthritis years earlier, I knew that I had the power to conquer and reverse PTSD and the other medical conditions too. I desired mental and physical health, and I was going to get it someday, somehow, some way. The journey to healing and wholeness was long and tough, but very rewarding.

Nearly 18 months after I resigned, I learned multiple complaints had been filed against him. He also destroyed three senior women with nearly 25 years experience each. This is what I was trying to prevent, but his speed train kept moving long after my departure. Leadership failed our office and he created a hostile and toxic work environment.

After all of this, they "quietly" forced him to retire…with dignity. He wasn't ousted, but was given a ceremony with all the fan fair to "honor" his contributions to the organization over a 25+ year.

Ridiculous….but very common.

Detrimental Health Effects
PTSD is a stigma associated with military people, but over the past few years, I've met more non-military women with PTSD than military women. They were harassed too, but stayed in jobs too long until they developed a mental or physical disease (dis-ease in the mind and body).

They stayed in positions where they consumed the hate of others and then, became it. They became hate and anger, and are now classified as nasty women or other unflattering names that people call women of power or strength.

Women are suffering from debilitating medical conditions that are created by hostile work environments, but can't leave because they need the medical benefits. Autoimmune diseases, such as: cancer, high blood pressure, hyperthyroidism, lupus, arthritis, and fibromyalgia are stress related conditions. We are working ourselves into body bags and wheelchairs.

Devalued To The Point Of No Value
Working in a hostile environment, over an extended period of time, affects your self-image and the ability to value yourself. When

that happens, you lose your ability to see your true value in the job market.

At certain times in my career, people offered me a job every month. Executives from oil companies and other government agencies would ask, "Christy, how long are you going to stay here? I would love to hire you to come and be on my team." Since resigning, I've been offered over 30 jobs.

I always thought if I continued to work just as hard and continue to exceed their expectations, that one day, I would be accepted in my organization. One day, they would see me as an equal. One day, I would get a high enough position and would no longer have to "prove" that I was worthy of respect. I would have earned it. But, that one-day never came.

It was a slow corrosion of my soul and self-image. Surrendering my preferences and values in order to fit into a box on a performance review. I continued to adjust and walk on eggshells for a period of time to suit the different personalities of the men I worked for. Dancing to the beat of a drum that was foreign to my ears. I assimilated into a white male dominated work environment, and gave up who I was to fit into an organization that wasn't designed for me to succeed in.

For the most part, I lost the ability to see my value because they squeezed it out of me, day after day, comment by comment, dirty look by dirty look, non-salute by non-salute. They slowly worked to break all that was good in me. My full value as a strong black woman. They worked and squeezed and pressed until…everything that I thought about my value was distorted and wrapped up in how they perceived my value. I was too afraid to leave.

When it comes to some high performers, there are two types of people. You have the professional side (the Rockstar), and the personal side (inner-being).

When you're harassed and bullied, the person who shrinks is the inner being. Your professional persona can be 400 feet tall, but the inner being can shrink to two feet tall. So, when it's time to make a decision to leave a job, the person that's making the decision is not the professional "Rock star" towering in self-confidence. It's the inner being that's tiny, wounded and confused.

Can you make the decision to leave if your inner being is wounded and paralyzed? Why do you stay?

When Will Enough Be Enough?

There are a lot of women who want to change, and then there are few that actually take ACTION to change. Let me be the first to admit that taking absolute responsibility for the undesired results and changing to correct and/or mitigate the results has been excruciating. Excruciating, but LIBERATING!!!

Do you know that you're digging your own grave, and you don't know where to start? Have you become a victim of your own success? Do you wear Golden Handcuffs and can't change because you've created a lifestyle around the job that's killing you? Are you ready to have a conversation and get clarity on your life?

If this is you, I want to offer you love, peace, joy, and light. Know that you are not alone. It's not too late to have the life that you've always dreamed of. It's not too late to FEEL the way you thought you would feel when you got high levels of success, but it's going to take working on yourself.

You've worked hard, bled, fought and cried for where you are today and all that you have. You've broken barriers and kicked doors open that were closed to you. You've set the example for women around you, and changed the trajectory of your family for generations to come. You've done the impossible.

Now, it's time to be whole. It's time for you to have inner-peace. It's time for you to have joy. It's time for you to love yourself. It's time for you to own all you've accomplished. It's time for you have a love that will set your soul on fire.

From everything I've learned over the past five years, I created a private community called "Women's Leadership Mastery with Christy." Check it out at **www.wlmwc.com** and get on the path to living the life that you desire.

To Your Success!!

My Advice For You...

1. Meditate for 5 minutes a day. It not only lowers blood pressure but can amp up your immune system while improving your ability to concentrate. There are tons of meditation apps and videos on YouTube. Give chanting or Om's a try to vibrate the negative energy off you. It takes time to train your mind to slow down, so be patient. If you can't sit in silence, try guided meditations.

2. Exercise at least 3 times a week. The challenge of having anxiety and being stressed out is it makes you tired and crave unhealthy food. When you're tired, you don't have the energy to work out, but working out gives you energy and reduces your stress. Eating sweet and salty foods, and not working out, creates a cycle and leads to weight gain. Make an effort to work out regularly.

3. Walk. Go for a 30-minute walk, without music or cell phone distractions, at least 3 times a week. This will give you an opportunity to get clarity on your life, reset, relieve your head pressure, and get some fresh air. One benefit of walking was my chronic lower back pain (8+ years) disappeared after 3 months.

4. Forgive someone. Buddha states, "Holding on to anger is like drinking poison and expecting the other person to die." We feel like forgiving others relieves them of what they did. It's actually the opposite and has absolutely nothing to do with the other person. Forgiveness relieves you of the burden and allows you to drop the excess baggage. They aren't carrying the baggage, and the toxic emotions (hate, anger, guilt, resentment), YOU ARE.

5. Monthly massages. Massages shouldn't be seen as a luxury or a treat. Massages should be a medical necessity, especially if you're in a hostile work environment. It's a way to release the negative and stored energy out of your body, and will reduce your chances of disease. Having regular massages will significantly lower heart rate, cortisol and insulin levels. All of this will help reduce daily stress.

Chapter 4

Eagles Soar
By Valorie Parker Hagen

Moving to South Florida from New York City in 1980, was a transition for me. I was newly married and was told that I could transfer from the corporate headquarters in Manhattan to the headquarters in South Florida. I had eight years with the company and received exemplary praise from everyone in management.

Constantly assured that I would be able to work in the corporate office of a mega department store prior to the move, I felt good. I spoke to the managers in South Florida and they were excited about my transfer and the value I added to the company with my work ethic.

I arrived in Fort Lauderdale and was early for my introductory meeting. I strongly believe to be on time is late, but early is on time. After informing the receptionist of my name, she went to the back to inform the manager of my arrival. It took a long time for her to return, but I didn't think anything of it.

When she returned, she told me to fill out a job application, and that someone would be with me shortly. I said okay and it didn't set off any alarms because I thought it was the company's policy so they could have my information, including my new address.

However, when I went to meet with the manager, it wasn't who I'd been talking to for the months preceding my arrival. It was someone totally different and after interviewing me, they told me that unfortunately, I was unable to get the job previously promised because I didn't have retail experience. I told her that I never had to do retail in my previous job, and the new job promised didn't entail retail.

Due to my resistance, they set up an interview for me at the store with another supervisor, and I reluctantly agreed. When I arrived, I was very uncomfortable. It was in the Galleria, a very high-end mall, and the looks I got from the other employees were very demeaning. As I talked to the supervisor, she told me that she didn't have a place for me. As I looked around, the other employees were Caucasian and looked like models, so I did not fit in at all.

That was my first experience of discrimination in the workplace. While talking to them on the phone, they couldn't tell my ethnicity. Also, coming from the main office in New York, they just assumed that I was anything other than African American because of my various skills and high-level recommendations.

You don't know what you don't know. Being from New York, I didn't have a clue about racial discrimination. When you work in an environment that doesn't encourage discrimination, you don't know what it feels like.

Something else I learned the hard way was I thought that the women would have my back because we were all sisters, sharing the common goal of trying to survive in a male-dominated environment. I never thought that other women would do that to me.

I decided not to fight anymore or play their game and walked away. I knew my value and that I was worthy of a job because of the skill sets I had developed throughout my career. I was very experienced and held management positions because of my talent, not because of the color of my skin.

With my head held high, I began filling out applications everywhere in corporate America. Within two weeks, I got a job at a prominent bank. I was thrilled because the job I was offered was a loan-servicing clerk and it was really out of my league.

I didn't know exactly what it was, but I knew I was going to excel at it. I wasn't going to power down or not be open to the new possibilities. I fit into the culture of the bank easily because I was always polished in my appearance, clothes, and communication. I learned very quickly and performed exceptionally well, while again, receiving rave reviews from everyone in management.

One day, I went to work and they told me that I needed to pull all my files because they had to be audited. I told them no problem and spent the next few days pulling all the files they requested. Of the nearly five people in management, I was the only one of color.

The auditors arrived and went through my files, finding my work to be in order. Impressed, they started asking me questions about how long I'd been in banking. I told them less than six months and then, they asked if I had been a bank teller prior to becoming a loan officer clerk, and I said no. Needless to say, they were impressed.

They were all Caucasian male suits, and I wasn't intimidated because of my experience in New York. Two days later, they called me into the office and said they had to let me go. Shocked, I asked my supervisor what I did wrong. Did I talk too much to the auditors? I didn't understand the reason.

She said, "No, that's not it. They were amazed at your work."

She started to chuckle and said, "You didn't really think that you were going to work here long term did you?"

I said, "Yes."

Then, she told me point blank, "We needed to meet our quota for affirmative action and you were the best candidate."

I was floored and couldn't believe how bold she was when she said it. She didn't even blink. As a consolation to walk away, they offered me two weeks' vacation pay, a week's salary, and a letter with exemplary reviews of my work so I could find employment somewhere else.

I have never felt as humiliated as I did at that moment. I heard about discrimination in elementary and high school when they taught about Dr. Martin Luther King fighting for desegregation. However, because of the diversity in New York, I never felt suppressed or oppressed.

My family taught me to love myself and respect others that have rule over you. The discrimination in Florida was something new and felt very foreign to me. I knew in order for me to be successful in a new area, I had to learn how to deal with it.

Life Lessons

What I've learned since those experiences is, women subconsciously put in more time at work. We do more than what's required because we don't want our male counterparts to think we can't handle the job because we are women, wives or mothers. But in reality, I have brothers and a husband…and I can tell you that when they are sick, the world stops! We keep it moving through illnesses and emotional issues.

Marianne Williamson says it best in her poem, *Our Deepest Fear*. She said, "Your playing small does not serve the world. There is nothing enlightened about shrinking so that other people won't feel insecure around you."

We should never ever let someone's opinion of us dictate our reality. As women, we are far greater than we know, and we are the most resilient creatures on the planet. We are the only unique creatures that have two wombs. One natural, to bring life into existence and one spiritual, that allows us to birth dreams from our knees into reality to allow men to accomplish their greatest accomplishments.

From the beginning of time, we were always called upon to make contributions to mankind. From biblical times to NASA, as demonstrated in the movie, "Hidden Figures." We've always been making things happen.

I encourage all my Queens, friends and family, regardless of color. We have far too many battles to fight, so let's not fight each other. We've been making it happen with oppositions such as sexual harassment, discrimination, domestic violence, cancer and more. Don't lose focus, and know that your dreams are far bigger than you are, and we have a lot more work to do.

We don't have to be employees. We have the smarts, talents, and skills to run our own companies and hire as we will, but our hands must be clean. We must operate without hatred, bitterness, strife, and envy.

Remember, Eagles always soar, so let's celebrate the beauty and talents of one another, and let's get the MONEY!

My Advice For You...

It's all about you and the lives you will affect. Iron can only sharpen iron if you are connected to a power source greater than your own. Always remember to keep God first in your life. If you are not a believer, there is one thing I know, when things get hard, the first thing we do is call out, "My God," or "Oh God."

So regardless of what you say, this lets me know that subconsciously, you believe in something other than yourself.

Below are some keys that I offer you for everyday life:

L - Love yourself so that you can love others

O - Own your space and take ownership of who you are and what you do.

V - Visualize yourself in a higher place spiritually, mentally and financially

E - Embrace the journey ahead without fear

Chapter 5

Someone Is Going To Remind You That You're Black, Baby
Jade Brown Russell

"The best way is always through." ~ Robert Frost

It was the summer of 2003, and I was headed to my first job fresh out of law school. I had been recruited by Stern and Arnold[1], one of the top law firms in the world. I was straight out of Southern University, a Historically Black College and University (HBCU) in Baton Rouge, LA. However, Michael, the attorney who recruited me to the firm, was totally committed to diversity.

When I arrived for my internship interview the prior summer, I stood on the 39th floor looking out at the Chicago skyline, and Michael greeted me saying, "Tame the New Orleans accent, stop looking out that window like you've never seen anything like this before, and act like you belong here!" The firm had a diversity program that yielded a handful of young, hungry and clueless brand new Black attorneys from HBCUs for its incoming class of 90 (mostly pale, male) attorneys. Most of my counterparts were from Ivy League and top-tier law schools like Harvard, Stanford and University of Chicago, and had fathers or grandfathers (or both) who were attorneys.

When I showed my daddy, a high school principal, my offer letter for $125,000 as a first-year attorney, he paused before looking up at me, and with a little shock and a lot of pride, he said, "Damn

---

[1] *Names have been changed to protect those who never even knew their innocence could be questioned!*

girl, that's more than I've ever made!" My mama, on the other hand, had a little bit of a different approach to life. So, when I shared my offer letter with her, she said something to me that has stayed with me since and always will. She has always been an honest mother – even when it hurts. "Just know that someone is going to remind you that you're Black, baby." And they did. And it hurt like hell. But, it was necessary.

My goal for sharing this story is definitely for the free therapy that I'm giving myself! Sometimes, you have to think back and remind yourself how much crap God carried you through. However, even more, I hope to give you hope that whatever you're going through now might hurt like a whole new Hell – but it's necessary.

* * * * *

It was my first day at the new firm. I was joining the Corporate Transactions Group. This group handled mergers, acquisitions, and securities regulatory transactions. I had a passion for the work, but honestly, didn't know the first thing about anything, even remotely related to the type of work these attorneys were handling. There were less than a dozen women in a group of about 100. And I was the only Black – unless you count Thomas who was biracial, and could pass for white and never admitted that he was Black. But, I'm from New Orleans, and I've seen plenty of what we call, "passé blanc folk".

The first day was filled with logistics. I was taken to my new office and introduced to my new secretary, Arnel, who would become my greatest ally. I was also connected with my associate and partner level mentors. My associate mentor was Jennifer, who later turned out to be the attorney that introduced me to the concept of all-nighters at the office (a story for a little later).

I learned a lot about work ethic from Jennifer, but it was on my very first day that she'd give me what I later learned was the advice that every woman joining the group received on their first day. We were sitting in Jennifer's small office, and she bluntly told me,

"Don't have a kid until you make partner. You won't be able to raise them. If you aren't already married, wait. If you are married, there's a high likelihood that you'll be divorced by the time you make partner."

There are three female partners in this group. Linda is about to get a divorce. Cathy is 45 and has a three and five year old, and Sara is an over 50 lesbian who just adopted a kid from Africa."

For the record, I sincerely believe that it was not Jennifer's intent to crush my dreams. This was her way of telling me how to survive – and she wasn't making this stuff up. Linda, Cathy, and Sara were all exactly as she described.

That day, I was also introduced to my partner mentor, Karim, who later turned out to be the pivotal reason I left the firm. He was a super smart, Arab man in his 50s. I walked into his office to introduce myself, and unlike Jennifer's office, it was huge and he had what seemed to be a dozen photos of his kids and grandkids, sprawled throughout his office.

He, too, gave me what seemed to be great advice on my first day – advice that actually has helped to shape one of the basic principles that I still live by today. "None of this sh*t is *THAT* important. At the end of the day, none of this is *THAT* important." By the end of my first day, I was confused. Did I mention that I knew absolutely nothing and was making $125,000?! I was confused, but I was also scared to death of failing.

The good news is I learned a lot at Stern. Despite my initial ignorance, I was relentless about learning everything I could about M&A and securities regulatory law. But, I was learning it on my own. My secretary, Arnel, often dropped books on my desk and said, "Here, read this book. Kevin read this when he first started." Kevin was a senior partner that Arnel also provided administrative support for. The bad news is, I couldn't read fast enough to keep up with the pace of the work that was coming my way. But, I survived and was grateful for her level of care.

* * * * *

About a year after I started, I got married. I flew out of Chicago on a Wednesday night with my laptop and KeyFob for remote access to all my work. I didn't tell anyone that I was getting married. I just kept hearing Jennifer's first day advice in my head. So, I worked all day Thursday and Friday, except for the rehearsal and dinner, and we got married on a Saturday. No honeymoon. I was back on a plane on Sunday, and back in the office on Monday.

Less than a year later, I found out I was pregnant. I knew something was up because I was constantly exhausted, and I couldn't stop using the restroom! So, I left the office for lunch and walked to a nearby pharmacy and got a pregnancy test. Right there in the office bathroom, I learned that I was pregnant. Like getting married, I held on to this information for as long as I possibly could because of Jennifer's first day advice.

I worked like crazy and as I mentioned earlier, Jennifer introduced me to all-nighters. She and I worked on an acquisition for two months straight, and we would literally rotate nights for who would stay all night and "turn changes" in the transaction documents for the next morning. So, nearly every other night, I was at the office all night.

Jennifer had no idea that I was pregnant. The day that the deal signed, we wrapped up at 5:30 a.m. I watched the sun rise and thanked God that it was finally over. Jennifer called me and told me that I had done a great job on the deal. She said, "Go home, get some rest, and let's get back here for…let's say 8:30 a.m."

"Wait, what?"

Yes, Jennifer wanted to get back the next morning to start working on the closing documents – we'd only signed the deal, not closed it. I remember going back to my apartment, showering and sitting up watching the morning news in fear that if I laid down to rest, I would not make it back to the office. I got back to the office for 8:30 a.m. and we had a 9:00 a.m. call with Linda, who was the partner working the deal. She was on "vacation" in Italy, but still working this huge deal.

I have never been so tired in my life, even to this day. I sat in Jennifer's office on a conference call with Lisa that morning and literally felt my head drop as I nodded off. When the call was over, I informed Jennifer that I was going to head to the Starbucks across the street, and offered to bring her something back. "No, I don't do caffeine, I just have a natural adrenaline that keeps me going," she explained. I was speechless.

Once I started showing, I finally went to Michael, the partner who recruited me to come to the firm. Michael was one of four black partners at the firm – all of them were men – but he wasn't in my group. He practiced Real Estate. I was absolutely terrified, thinking he'd be disappointed in me.

I figured Jennifer's first day advice was common knowledge -- usually unspoken, but common knowledge nonetheless. But, Michael calmed my fears saying, "Brown, you know you are not the first woman to have a baby, you know!" He helped me navigate the process of delivering the news to my group heads. And we all carried on – business as usual.

My doctor decided to induce my labor on January 17th. I worked until January 16th, carrying my blackberry into the delivery room with me. I took 12 weeks of maternity leave before returning back to work, and it seemed that everything returned to "normal." I exhaled and was proud of myself for defying the odds – for denying Jennifer's notion that women couldn't be mothers and wives while still getting the work done.

* * * * *

And then, in what seemed like a split second, I found myself picking up my five-month-old daughter at midnight from the firm's subsidized "after hour's daycare" because my husband, who was also from New Orleans, was homesick, and spent more time back at home during the summer months. I was working on a new deal with my mentor, Karim, and it required more of my time and attention. I was excited to be working with my mentor and felt like I could learn so much from him to help me finally close that self-admitted knowledge gap.

Not long after we started working the deal, I noticed that Karim frequently asked if I was sure that I had enough time to devote to the project. I assured him that I had the time and capacity to do the work. At this point, I was a third-year associate, and made $150,000 a year. Prior to having my daughter, I'd been working my butt off to try to learn everything that I could as fast as I could, but it still wasn't enough.

I've learned that one of the most compromising positions you can find yourself in is when you don't know what you don't know. I found myself standing in that position for the first time in my life. There I was, a physically and mentally exhausted third year, black associate from Southern University (a third tier law school), who was married with a five month old baby. One could easily argue that the odds were not stacked in my favor. And then, I screwed something up on Karim's project, but he never said a word about it to me. Looking back on it now, I can share that it wasn't a huge screw up, but it was just enough.

Instead of saying something directly to me in the form of constructive criticism, Karim said nothing, but managed TO DO a lot. What Karim managed to do, was create one of the most unhealthy work environments that I've ever been in. The man who was my mentor – the man who I longed to learn from – the one partner that I should have been able to screw up something with, because I would be assured that he'd help show me the right way, never said a word to me about it.

You may be thinking…this doesn't seem like harassment. It wasn't. You may be thinking that it doesn't seem like a hostile work environment. – you just screwed up, Jade! You're right. It may not fall into the hostile category either. But, it certainly became a toxic working environment.

Although Karim never breathed a word about the situation to me, he felt that only a black person could speak to me about this matter. So, he went to Chris, one of the black partners, so that *he* could talk with me. Karim expressed his concerns to Chris that with a new baby, I may not be able to balance the workload, and he felt that Chris was in a better position to talk to me about this screw up than he was as my "mentor."

Chris was not in my group. He was in the Insurance Group, so he was totally clueless about the type of work I was doing. He was not my recruiter. I had never worked on anything with him. His sole qualification for being identified by Karim as the most suitable candidate to have a "conversation" with me was that he was black. The day Chris called me into his office to talk was the day I heard my mother's words replay in my head. I heard her say, "Just know that someone is going remind you that you're Black, baby." Now, for the first time in my professional career, that someone had a name – Karim.

That day in his office, Chris "*confidentially*" shared Karim's "*concern*" that I couldn't manage the workload with a new baby. Karim even shared with Chris that because of my Southern University roots, I was already behind my peers, and it would be almost impossible to catch up with them. Chris tried to calm my fears by telling me that I wasn't being pushed out. It was about two weeks before the Christmas holiday, and he assured me that I was still going to get my $50,000 bonus based on my work during the year. But, he was clear that I couldn't afford another screw up. I walked out of Chris' office and wasn't sure whether I wanted to cry, scream or fight.

The following days were quiet for me, but I assumed (which I was wrong) that it was that way for everyone. Year-end is one of the busiest times of year for a transactional attorney because all of your clients are trying to close their deal in the current year. Everyone else was busy closing their deals, and in an instant, I went from being swamped to having no work at all.

However, I got a call from another white partner in my group who said, "Hi, Jade. Listen, I have a client who is based in New Orleans and they're looking for an Associate General Counsel, and I thought you might be interested since that's your hometown. I know it's been a challenge for you since returning from maternity leave. I just wanted to put it on your radar."

I felt totally deflated because that's not what I wanted. I wanted to be the first black female to make partner in my group – even if it took me eight years to do it. I also felt absolutely ashamed because I wondered how this partner heard that things had been "challenging." It was confirmation that conversations were being had all around me.

* * * * *

With everything that I was experiencing in such a short time at the office, I felt like there was no way for me to win at Stern, so I made the most of my holiday break in New Orleans. I hired a headhunter, and was offered several jobs in a matter of days. I decided to take one of those jobs because I knew that I was not set up to succeed at Stern, and even the slightest oversight, typo or infraction on my part, would be scrutinized with a magnifying glass for the remainder of my days there. I resolved in my mind that operating in constant fear was not a way to build a career – at least not MY career.

On January 3rd, I returned to the office after the New Year's holiday, and went directly back to Chris (as my assigned Black interpreter), and informed him that I was leaving the firm. Chris seemed shocked, but he definitely didn't try to talk me out of it either. I think he was more shocked at how quickly I responded to our prior conversation, as it had only been two weeks since I sat in his office. I asked Chris to let Karim know of my departure since Karim had chosen him to be our go-between. I never spoke to Karim about me leaving – never said goodbye.

My last day at the firm was January 17th, my daughter's first birthday. Through her tears, Arnel helped me pack up my office. She said that she thought I was "the one." I asked Arnel if she thought me having a kid made a difference in the end, and she just dropped her head. I made my rounds to see all the folks that I "grew up" with at the firm.

My last stop was my exit interview. My group head was the partner who conducted my exit interview. I didn't mention a single word about my experience because I figured, I was no different than anyone else who'd been "coached" out, pushed out, or dragged out of the firm. I thought, "So, what was the point of even telling *my* truth?" And just like that, I was gone.

A year or so later, I received a call from a female student from my alma mater who'd been recruited to work at Stern. She was joining the same group that I'd departed from. She wanted advice on how to succeed at Stern. I gave her the same advice that Jennifer gave me on my first day. She didn't survive either. It was only then that I realized my silence made me just as guilty as Karim. My silence deprived a young Black woman who was just like me (for all intents and purposes) of an opportunity to excel in a place that I didn't.

It's true that many times, **CHAMPIONS NEVER TELL**, but today, I choose to speak about my experience because there is power in the tongue. There is also so much power in pain. Here are a few principles that I learned from my experience:

My Advice For You…

1. The best way is always through. I'm sure you've heard the phrase, "Everything that I need to know, I learned in kindergarten!" When I was in Mrs. Barzon's kindergarten class at McDonogh #39 Elementary in New Orleans, we'd often sing a song called, "I'm Going on a Bear Hunt." If you don't know it, Google it! It will change your life – seriously! The song goes:

We're goin' on a bear hunt,
We're going to catch a big one,
I'm not scared
What a beautiful day!
Oh look! It's a [*whatever obstacle you encounter*]!
Can't go over it,
Can't go under it,
Can't go around it,
Got to go through it!

This song taught me so much about life. First, you should know that there will be times in life when you will have to journey out to do something that's scary – like hunt down a bear! You will have no idea what's in store for you, but you have to know in your heart that whatever comes your way, you're going to get what you came for, and it's going to be huge!

Even when you are scared as hell, you must constantly remind yourself that you are not scared because you are whatever you say you are. And when you encounter whatever obstacles you will ultimately face (because they will definitely avail themselves), you must know that you will be better because of them. I couldn't go over, under or around the issues that I faced at Stern.

As hurtful as those issues seemed at the time, the lesson, the blessing, the beauty of it all was in me going through it. For those of you who are not brave enough to sing children's songs to yourself (in your head or out loud), you can change the words up a bit. Try changing *"bear hunt"* to *"faith walk,"* and watch God change your mind about some things!

2. Don't let someone talk you out of it before you even start. On my very first day at Stern, I let Jennifer talk me out of success. Don't have kids. Don't get married. Prepare for divorce. And in those moments when those things happened to me, you better believe that I was subconsciously telling myself that I wouldn't make it. I don't blame Jennifer for what I perceived to be my failure at Stern. Her first day pep talk turned out to be one of the greatest lessons I learned there.

The truth is, because of the weight I put in her words, I was doomed before I ever started. Folks will flat out tell you what you can't do, because they believe that they can't do it. Don't let someone who gave up on their dreams – of having kids, getting married, and making partner – talk you out of yours. Today, I give myself that "first day" pep talk (it's not always on the first day), and it usually starts with, "I'm going on a faith walk...!"

3. Never put yourself in a position where you have to be reminded who you are. My mother's words, as I considered my first job offer, transcended that moment. Her words transcended race and gender, too. After practicing law for 14 years, I now know the power of knowing who you are. I am also keenly aware of the pain that comes when you leave it to someone else to remind you.

I measure myself according to what I know about myself – *who* I come from (spiritually and naturally), *where* I come from, and *what* I am capable of. I will never allow myself to be measured by someone else's yardstick.

4. Every square counts. When I was at Stern, Karim's first day advice to me was, "None of this sh*t is *THAT* important. At the end of the day, none of this is *THAT* important." The truth is *ALL* of this sh*t is *THAT* important. Be reminded that God plays chess, not checkers. In chess, you have six different types of pieces, each with specific rules on how they move and can be played in the game. Only half of the board is utilized in checkers. The player skips every other square. In chess, every square counts. Every job, every opportunity, every experience, every struggle, every sacrifice, every hater, every joy-stealer and every "no" – God assures us that they all count.

Steve Jobs once said, "You can't connect the dots looking forward – you can only connect the dots looking back." You have to go through it – whatever it was, it was necessary! Many times, we can't see how much these squares are worth, but they are often tools of motivation and inspiration.

So, what does that mean? It means that you can't fail! It means that even when it looks like failure and feels like failure, it's just another square. It's just a part of a bigger strategy God has for your life. Let God make his move! Every moment, every square counts. Every second of my experience at Stern counted, and it has made all the difference in my life today. *ALL* of that sh*t was *THAT* important!

5. Squad up. I can honestly say that there were moments when I didn't know whether I could survive. There were days when I would sit and say, "Jade, what are you doing to yourself?" I literally felt like I lost myself, because the truth is sometimes, you don't realize that you're actually drowning when you're trying to be everyone else's anchor – your kids, your spouse, your work, or family. I'm here to encourage you!

The stresses of work, motherhood, and marriage, you can survive it – you just can't do it alone. The truth is, you have to surround yourself with a strong squad who will help keep you afloat. Your squad will be family who will be your kiddie coverage on long nights or date nights. Your squad will be your friends who plan a girls' night, because you are all living the same thing and you all need it. Your squad will be the ones who know that even an anchor needs to be checked on and cared for sometimes.

Get yourself a squad, because only a strong squad understands that sinking is not an option.

Chapter 6

Crabs In A Barrel Mentality
By VonGretchen Nelson

It was just two days before Thanksgiving, I was told by an African-American female (Renee), that I was not fulfilling her needs in my current role, and I only had 40 days before my position was going to be eliminated. I was floored, emotionally distraught, and highly confused. I'm a professional woman with over 18 years of Human Resource experience. What just happened?

During my tenure, I was not given a performance review. I did not have any meaningful conversations about my position, nor was offered any interventions. I was not offered a mentor, sponsor or coach. Every scheduled performance discussion was either rescheduled or cancelled, and a lateral move was not considered before Renee made the decision to terminate my employment. I needed answers.

The Background

My direct manager, Renee, was an African-American female who was on maternity leave when an African-American male, Joel, hired me. Renee didn't partake in the hiring process for my position. The first two months in my position was smooth sailing. Joel was the interim director who displayed all the skills of a confident, successful and transparent manager. Joel exhibited leadership skills to ensure the success of everyone on the team. I knew, in my heart, I made the right decision to leave my former employer, and was extremely satisfied with my new employer under Joel's leadership.

Fast-forward to the first of the year when Joel was released from his duties and Renee returned to her position after maternity leave. I immediately sent an email to Renee introducing myself and welcoming her back. It took her over a month to respond to my email. During the six-week wait, many of my colleagues (mostly white women) asked me if I've met or spoken to Renee. My response was "No," and they all responded one of three ways: 1) A long sigh 2) A glaring stare or 3) I can't wait for y'all to meet.

Renee and I finally met at a partnership event seven weeks later. When I saw her, I walked up to her with the biggest smile and my hand extended to introduce myself. Lo and behold, she simply walked past me to talk to someone else she recognized. Only after chatting with them, she turned and gave me a nonchalant apology and said it was nice to meet with a "straight face."

My first impression of Renee was forever set in stone. It was clear she didn't like me without even taking the time to get to know me. At that moment, I was determined to develop a healthy working relationship by any means necessary. My career was the most important thing to me.

Please, Like Me

Whenever you are in a position as a grown adult female and your goal is to make someone like you, especially someone that looks like you, chances are the outcome will not be beneficial or healthy. I found myself stressing about everything, no matter how big or small it seemed. I reached out to several African-American women about my anxiety due to workplace stress, and shared the embarrassing story about my twenty-five-pound weight gain since joining the firm. All of their responses were the same, "**RUN!**"

I love what I do for a living. I was coaching, developing, and training individuals to be the best version of themselves in the workplace. Time and time again, I've coached employees and managers to bring their authentic selves to work, but I quickly realized I was not taking my own advice. The months ahead were some of the worst in my entire life. I dreaded coming to work. My immediate supervisor did not like me before we met, and it was clear she wanted me to know it.

Silos vs. Champions In The Workplace

I found myself trying to enter workplace silos. Silos are extremely unhealthy and are a direct reflection of a poor team management. I didn't want to be the "angry black woman" or the "bitter and disgruntled employee." With a team of eight employees, we had three different silos. I tried to fit into all of them, but it didn't work because I quickly learned that we all wanted to fight for Renee's recognition, attention, and approval. I wanted to have a great working relationship with all of my team members. I've never been one that worked well in silos, so why try now?

As one of the senior managers on the team, my conversations and demeanor changed with my colleagues. I wasn't as out going on the conference calls or in-person meetings. I wasn't as vocal with my thoughts and ideas related to our mission, vision, and objectives. I did the required qualifications of my job description, and didn't go the extra mile to "fit in" or to be "liked" by Renee. This indirectly caused my demise in the workplace and eventually, I was terminated.

Once I realized my behavior was a direct reflection of Renee's intimidation, a light bulb went off. I remember being in meetings and being rudely interrupted by her, or have ideas totally dismissed. What was so infuriating, many times **MY** "dismissed" ideas were presented by her to the senior leaders without me knowing, or her attributing those ideas to me.

I exhibited profound knowledge and leadership skills that exceeded expectations at this point in my career. Apparently, it just wasn't good enough for Renee's team. I have never experienced such humiliation, and felt so worthless in my career. I lost the respect of my colleagues because I wasn't the same inspiring and forward-thinking person they met before Renee's return. I needed to make a change for myself that didn't depend on whether someone liked me or not.

I wanted to remove myself from the quick sand but I wasn't even sure where to start. One of my greatest skills is that I've always been great at networking. I asked Renee over 10 times for a sponsor, coach or mentor, but the requests were rejected or ignored. She said finding a mentor or sponsor was time consuming, and she had more important things to do. So, I decided to take control of my destiny.

I started inviting senior leaders within the company to coffee meetings, lunch meetings or office meetings. The response was overwhelmingly positive. During our conversations, many questions were answered without me going into detail. More than half of the people I met knew Renee, and gave me advice for dealing with her personality type. I only shared a very small percentage of our issues, and blamed a lot of the challenges on access to technology.

The senior leaders and I had some very powerful conversations, and they left a lasting impression on me. They assisted me with my overall goal of being the best version of myself at work. I walked away with the support of people who would later become my champions. Everyone should have at least five champions.

My Sista

During each conversation, I found myself protecting Renee without her knowledge. I blamed the lack of access to integrated technology as the issue. I spent 11 months in a position where Renee didn't grant me full system access to perform the duties of my role. Why was I defending "my sista" who clearly didn't give a damn about me?? What did this say about me?

I come from a blended family. I'm one of 12 children. I've always been the foundation for many of my family and friends. Yes, I was the Super Hero. Even with experiencing pain and despair at work, I put on my professional cape. Renee received some of the highest praises from me, even as she continued to treat me poorly. She didn't have a clue how proud I was of her from the moment I discovered an African-American woman was in command of an important department of a very large firm.

If one of us shines, we all shine. Why couldn't she understand that? Why couldn't she treat me with the same level of respect that I gave to her? Black women are a powerful force, but we do more harm working *against* each other than we do working *with* one another. There's so much opportunity in the world for all of us to WIN! We don't have to pull each other down to build ourselves up. I'm not built that way, and that's why I was having such a challenging time working for "my sista."

Work Journal

After seeking counseling for severe anxiety due to workplace trauma, my counselor told me to start a work journal. I laughed at the idea because I could never write everything down because, by 2 p.m., I was so exhausted from meetings I just wanted to lay down, cry and simply forget everything about that day. After a few discussions about the work journal with my counselor, I decided to do it. Despite my initial hesitation, I must admit, it changed my life!

Week after week, I started writing down all the good and dreadful things that happened during the workday. I started to list the names of people who could help me, but I was too afraid and mostly ashamed to ask for help. I wrote down names of people who called to simply say hello. I kept a record of people who started a conversation with a "Good Morning" or "Nice to see you again." I kept a record of things that I did well, and identified areas of opportunity.

I liked this concept so much, until I started to recall conversations and interactions over the year, and quickly realized how depressed I was during that time due to workplace harassment, bullying, and the overall toxic work environment. I was emotionally drained. My kids were lacking a full-time parent, because I was so depressed and was sleeping the evenings and weekends away. Every conversation was centered around Renee and her feelings. What about me? What do I want?

Here's an example of a few items from my work journal during my time at 3Firm, Inc.:

Name/Topic	Month	Situation
Renee	January	Renee returned to work and sent the team an email
VonGretchen C. Nelson	January	Requested an introductory meeting with Renee & discuss her vision for my role.
VonGretchen C. Nelson	February	Sent an email to Renee with nine questions about my role. Ask about Renee's work style and how do she hold her team accountable? Renee never acknowledge the email.
Renee	February	Received an email from Renee asking me to text or call her because she rarely responses to emails.
Renee	February	Renee informed me that she was planning to schedule meetings with everyone on the team to discuss goals and objectives for the reminder of the year.
Renee	February	Renee sent me an email and asked me to "grab" time on her calendar to talk about my goals.
Renee	February	Renee cancelled our meeting hours before we met and said that she wanted to replace the meeting and discuss a project with another employee.
VonGretchen C. Nelson	March	Requested time for a 1on1 to discuss my position, career and opportunities within 3Firm Inc. Also, asked Renee (again) to help me identify a sponsor (senior leader). Renee never acknowledge the email.
Renee	March	Renee was non-responsive, so I sent her a calendar invite to discuss Career Counseling and Systems Access. Her calendar was free for 10am. She cancelled the meeting and it was never rescheduled.

VonGretchen C. Nelson	May	Worked with HR to complete a domestic transfer.
VonGretchen C. Nelson	June	Emailed Renee to get approval and a review of a critical project. Renee never acknowledge the email.
Performance Achievement	July	I received an email from Human Resources that supervisors were documenting feedback for team members, but I didn't receive anything. Renee never forwarded the information.
Renee	July	Renee worked very hard to find a mentor for a new Hispanic male hire. My mentor and sponsor requests were ignored.
VonGretchen C. Nelson	July	Asked Renee to participate on a new diversity initiative and she denied my request.
Renee	August	Renee said that she was concerned about my lack of follow-up and engagement with co-workers last week. I informed her that I was on vacation during her email requests.
Renee	August	Requested one on one with Renee to discuss my role and system's access to properly do my work. Renee never acknowledged the email.

Facts

After I wrote down the facts based on live conversations, email exchanges, or text communications, I quickly realized that Renee was setting me up for failure. The realization hit me hard that I would never be successful under her leadership. I was only one step away from her title, so did she feel threatened? Did I intimidate her? Was she jealous of me? What was it? Why was I treated with such disrespect from the time she returned to work?

The facts were listed in front of me. I didn't include all the details of the journal, because it's important to keep the name of the firm and manager confidential. The timeline was roughly 25 pages and my daily writing was over 100 pages. I also couldn't ignore the fact that my deteriorating health was directly related to my toxic work environment. Yes, I was terminated from the firm, but that should have never happened.

I never felt welcomed by Renee, and she got what she wanted in the end, my termination. I reached out to other leaders within the firm, but unfortunately, I was not selected for any of their open positions. I had favorable interviews, but once the internal manager's reference check was conducted, the hiring manager decided to select another person for the role. If Renee didn't want me on her team, why would she sabotage my career and prevent me from being hired for another position in the firm?

Relocation

I had plans to relocate back to South Carolina when I was first hired at 3Firm, Inc. Sadly, my grandmother died on April 5th (one month before I relocated) after a two-year battle with breast cancer. She died of heart failure. This was one of the most challenging times in my life. I had major trauma both professionally and personally. During the grieving process, I encountered some unforeseen issues with the relocation request. Renee gave me an extremely tough time relocating back to South Carolina.

Joel wrote a letter stating that he was aware of the relocation upon job offer, and he approved it. Joel also had to contact several departments to push my request through because Renee was blocking it. Finally, my relocation request was approved. I was moving away from the silos at the head office and all my work problems. At least, that's what I thought. South Carolina had so many surprises that I was not prepared for in the months ahead.

My Value

After relocating back to South Carolina, I began to discover what was important: God, my children, my health and my happiness. I was not valuing myself by staying in a position that caused thyroid flare-ups, tachycardia, migraines, hair loss and mood swings. I was diagnosed with clinical depression and had to start taking several different medications a day. I didn't receive the same training, support, respect, or opportunities as my white female counterparts from Renee. It was up to me to take control of my health and wealth.

After working in the Human Resources field for 18 years, I knew I had a lot to offer any department within the firm, so I decided to apply for other positions. For every applied position, I met the basic qualifications and desired skills. I felt great and confident that I was going to stay with 3Firm, Inc., but in a new role. I had no idea that Renee had plans to terminate me so quickly and provide horrible references.

I understood my value and obviously, 3Firm, Inc. did as well, because they offered me a very large severance package. I don't know the last time a company terminated someone due to performance, and offered a large severance. The day after my termination, I applied for a business license, and started my own Diversity & Inclusion Consulting Firm. It took me less than 48 hours to build my company's website. The colors (purple and teal) came to me in a dream, so I knew God was talking to me.

The tests I went through in the prior year, have now become my testimony. I am wiser. I am stronger. I am whole, because the hatefulness did not break me. Now, I have more mentors, sponsors, and champions than ever. I have people in positions of power who genuinely want to see me win, and I'm WINNING because I found my voice, again! If you want to win, stand on my shoulder. Let's get out of the crab barrel and win together.

My Advice For You...

1. Professional counseling. The counseling I received changed my life. My work journal helped me, both professionally and personally. I could see in black and white exactly what and who was driving me into a deep depression. "When you know better, you do better" is a very true old saying. I will never allow myself to miss out on opportunities because of wanting a manager or anyone to "like" me or constantly seek their approval. Rejection is a horrible feeling, and

I learned a valuable lesson, "My strengths do not come from man alone"!

2. Diversity of thought. I seek out clients and managers with great personalities, and welcome "diversity of thought" into the decision-making process. It increases the lines of communication and ultimately, the productivity of the organization. I refuse to be humiliated in front of my peers (again) by anyone who is lacking in their own areas, by pushing their weaknesses onto me. I refuse to allow myself to be in a position to allow anyone (regardless of title) to be dismissive, patronizing and disrespectful. 3Firm Inc. took a lot out of me, but I came through stronger than ever. I am a thriving business owner, and I know it's all because of the storm I went through.

3. Host Women Empowerment Seminars. Last year, I decided to host my first Women's Empowerment Seminar during the Christmas holiday in South Carolina. I welcomed 20 African-American women to my home, and we all brought the good, the bad and the ugly to the table. Each person was given a question and asked to reflect on their experience from that year. Everyone brought their authentic selves to the conversation.

We had plenty of tears flowing, tons of hugs that were met with great laughter. We talked about the loss of a loved one, losing a career, relationships, business owner woes, domestic abuse, networking and supporting each other, and so much more. I thought about Renee during this time, and wondered how our relationship could have been so much stronger if she had this type of support and circle of friends.

At that very moment, I realized that I was blessed beyond measure. I was so ashamed and afraid of my situation, and extremely embarrassed because I put away my cape. I'm about to host my second Empowerment Seminar in December, and I can't wait to hear the stories and knowing that I don't have to put on a mask with my sisters. We are all in this together!

4. Champions. Everyone should have at least five champions. Identify at least three professional champions, and two personal champions. These are the people who will sing your praises when you're not in the room. These people will become your cheerleaders and your life-long friends and references. Champions will have an extended network, and be extremely well connected in their industry of choice. Your Champions will speak highly of your character 24/7. They know your career aspirations and values. When selecting your Champion, ask yourself, "Does this person want me to WIN?"

Chapter 7

Is It Time To Call In The Law?
Ronetta Francis

You have been in the advertising/marketing field for years, and have just started working at a new ad agency. After receiving your commission check late two months in a row, you learn that Amy in the Accounting Department has made it known that she does not like processing the ad sales and commissions paperwork for the company's African-American employees. When you inquire about the status of your commission check, which is now two weeks late, she responds that she will get to it "when she can."

This confuses you because you know of other team members who have already received their commissions. Later, in the break room, you clearly hear Amy stating openly and loudly, with members of management present, "Can you believe that new uppity gal had the nerve to question me? Asking me when she was gonna get paid? Like I owed her an explanation at all. I swear, those N -ers are as stupid as they come. None of them know how to count. I always have to go over their work three to four times —especially the new ones — to make sure they have submitted the correct commissions. I don't care if it means holding up on paying out the commissions. Most times, it's right, but you just can't ever be too sure because there's no way they should be making that kind of money!"

Having to endure language and treatment such as this is nothing new. It's also nothing new for management to be aware of the mistreatment, and to condone it by not putting an end to the offensive language, or telling Amy that her language and behavior would not be permitted in the workplace, or better still, firing Amy on the spot. Too often, many people feel that they have no choice but to silently tolerate this type of treatment. Many have been conditioned, either through urban legend or past experiences, that to make waves, to report unacceptable, offensive and racist behavior, would be career limiting.

Whether it's common knowledge or not, Amy's behavior and the manager's failure to correct it would be considered a violation under federal employment laws. It is, in fact, against the law to engage in harassing — unwelcome — and conduct based upon an individual's race and gender, among other things, including national origin and age. If enduring the harassing behavior is necessary in order to continue working, or if it creates an environment that is toxic, hostile or abusive, it is also against the law.

Harassment is illegal when it is so frequent or severe that it creates a work environment that would be considered intimidating, hostile, or offensive — even to an objective, third person — or when it results in the employer taking an adverse employment action against the person who is the object of the harassment, such as the victim being fired or demoted.

While these laws are intended to cover the most serious behaviors, what that also means is that petty slights, annoyances, and isolated incidents (unless extremely serious) will not rise to the level of illegality. And while not rising to the level of illegality, this is just the sort of thing that can get under your skin, negatively impact your morale and job performance.

Illegal and offensive behaviors range from the obvious and absurd:

- Manager referred to African American employees as monkeys, demeaning them by stating, "You're lucky I pay you because back then, you did not get paid. Blacks work for free." (Phoenix aircraft fueling Company paid $250,000 to settle race harassment lawsuit);

- Employees used offensive and inflammatory language to refer to other employees of color ("wetback/beaner" - Hispanic employees; "wagon burner" — Native American employees; and "nigger" — African American employees). Management either minimized or ignored complaints by the employees. "Welcome to the oil fields, this is how we talk." - several of the employees who complained were demoted or fired. (Wyoming related oil-gas company settled race harassment lawsuit for $1.2 million);

- Transgendered employee was fired for not conforming to company's gender-based expectation (A Mississippi financial loan company was ordered to pay a $53,000 award in arbitration to resolve a sex discrimination lawsuit);

- Pregnant employees were told, "You are too pregnant to continue working. You are a liability. Had I known of your pregnancy, you would not have been hired. Aren't you ever going to quit having kids?" Company also denied reasonable accommodations, placing employees on involuntary unpaid leave. (New Mexico/Texas convenience store chain settled pregnancy and disability discrimination lawsuit for $950,000).

To the nuanced - nearly imperceptible

- Supervisors and managers engaging in hyper-scrutiny of work products/performance, failing to use the same barometer of performance for all team members.

- Changing schedules/assignments, either without notice to the employee or with full knowledge of the resulting scheduling or workload conflicts.

- Using biased language/code words such as, "You are so articulate. You're not anything like the other black people I see on the news. You are so intimidating/unapproachable"

- Assuming the women or people of color serve a subordinate or subservient role: client asking an African American female Senior Vice President to fetch a cup of coffee in business meeting.

The line between illegal, offensive conduct and otherwise legal, yet still, equally offensive and hostile behavior can make a difference in what remedies or relief you may be entitled to under the law. However, the blurrier that line is, the more likely employees are to endure a toxic work environment and consequently suffer physically, emotionally and financially.

MY STORY

Looking back over my professional legal career, it seems transparent - and almost predestined - that the trajectory and path of the practice of law was shaped in large part to an experience I had as a second-year law student. In law school, securing an internship at a law firm was the ultimate goal. The older and more prestigious the law firm, the better. The entire process remains highly competitive. To this day, students work to stand out from their peers. Some do just about anything to gain an advantage in obtaining and succeeding in prestigious law firm internships.

Why? Because these internships generally lead to official job offers after law school. To have a job waiting for you when you finish law school is every student's dream because attending law school is not cheap.

So, when I received a note to meet with the career advisor regarding an internship opportunity, I was overjoyed, to say the least. She asked me if I would be interested in working at this well-known firm. It was mid-Spring semester, an odd time to begin an internship, but I did not care at all. After I literally jumped at the job offer, the advisor shared with me that, to this law firm's credit, they were working to actively diversify their internship program.

I took from her carefully crafted words, that I had been considered and selected for this opportunity primarily because of the color of my skin. Initially shocked by the transparency, I overcame my hesitation and vowed that even if my race got me in the door, my intellect, work ethic and personality would keep me there.

I arrived at the firm, and was greeted with the expected grandeur of an established, prestigious law firm. When I saw the mahogany desks, the marble floors, the floor to ceiling windows, I was giddy — thinking, "This could be my life, as a lawyer. I could work here every day."

I met my assigned partner in the firm. He seemed nice enough, rather distant though. Then again, I didn't know what else to expect from a bankruptcy attorney. I didn't know much about bankruptcy law, so I knew I would have to approach this challenge head-on, and learn everything I could. I didn't plan on practicing bankruptcy law (yawn), but if I could impress this partner, then maybe he would recommend hiring me for some other area of the firm.

Next, they showed me where I would be working, and when I saw my designated workspace, I felt like I had been punched in the gut. You see, I was taken to the bankruptcy records file room. Initially, I thought this was just a stop on the grand tour, so that I would know where to go to pull the files that I needed to research the cases I would be working on. Then, came the sucker punch.

At the end of the last bookshelf and nestled in the back of the room, was a makeshift tabletop with a phone and a few office supplies. Slowly, it dawned on me…this was my workspace. It held none of the grandeur that the orientation tour had foretold.

Even though I was a legal neophyte, it did not escape me that everyone has to start somewhere — that there are dues to be paid/sacrifices to be made on the road to professional success. With humility as a deeply held personal value, I did not consider myself greater than my workspace, and certainly not greater than any other law school intern who had been previously hazed by these working conditions.

If this was to be the road I had to travel to get to the brass ring at the finish line, then, so be it. I had already invested time and money, and sacrificed sleep and a social life in pursuit of this legal degree, I was certainly not going to be derailed or distracted by a less than ideal workspace.

And since I had no frame of reference as what to expect, I internalized my disappointment, pushing it well below the surface. I settled in and got about the business of learning bankruptcy law so as to immediately add value in assisting the partners and associates in performing their legal duties, get that much coveted job offer and get the heck out of that file room.

Throughout the semester, everything seemed to be going very well. I received positive feedback from both the partner, the associates and other staff. I felt great — accomplished. Quite naturally, as the Spring semester was nearing its end, there was a lot of talk around the office about the upcoming summer intern class.

Considering no one had mentioned to me that my internship experience would end at the end of the spring semester, naïvely, I assumed that I would also be included in the summer class of interns. Yes!! Just to be clear, being part of a law firm's Summer Intern Class is the equivalent of making it to the Super Bowl — you're not quite yet the NFL Champion — but you are one step closer to that ultimate prize, for which you have worked and trained tirelessly to achieve.

The Summer Intern Class…this is the time when the law firms do all the wining and dining of the handpicked law students to whet their appetite for practicing law in a big firm, and to secure employment within their particular firm. With all the buzz around the office about the Summer Intern Class, I grew more and more excited. And since no one had mentioned anything about how my duties, assignments or workstation would change, I assumed that I would be included in this elite group. My thought was, keep on working until someone says otherwise. And so, I did.

Then one day at lunch, as I walked past the hallway leading to the bank of elevators, I saw them. This gaggle of blonde and brunette law students, all lacking in melanin, were being shepherded through the hallways of this prestigious firm with great merriment and laughter. I could still hear the light joviality as they entered the elevators and descended toward a delightful dining experience. THEY were the Summer Intern Class and I was not included.

Worse yet, there was never any intention to include me. I realized as I stood on the imported marbled floor, glaring at the brass elevator doors, which mirrored my disillusioned, crestfallen, and humiliated face, that I merely existed at that firm to allow them to feel good about themselves and their "progressiveness," as they checked the previously vacant diversity box.

I had never felt so devalued, so dehumanized, so disrespected in all my life. I was no longer a person, but a statistic. In that moment, all I wanted to do was to take the big box of boring a$$ bankruptcy files, and throw them into the face of the boring bankruptcy partner. But I could not, and would not do that. Because even as a law student, I was a professional.

The personal insignificance I felt each day I walked those halls was compounded by the fact that I could not and did not speak up for myself. Even though I knew with every fiber of my being that what I was experiencing was not right, I did not have it within me to shout, "This is not fair! You can't treat people like this!!"

I had no voice — so I told no one of this experience. I kept it to myself, mainly because I didn't want to jeopardize the $10 an hour I was being paid to work. And back in the early 1990s, that was a significant amount of money — money that I needed to support myself and my studies. I was utterly disgusted with myself, knowing that every dollar of that paycheck I spent on rent or groceries was paid with "blood money." Money earned at the expense of my heart, soul and humanity.

This feeling of plummeting self-worth deepened because I was reminded daily of how differently I was being treated from the other interns. For the entirety of the summer I had to walk past where Summer Interns Biff, Becky and the like (not really their names) worked — actual offices with windows and mahogany desks. Not only that, I had to hear about their wonderful lunches, dinners, entertainment, outings and connections, from which I was excluded. It never crossed anyone's mind, nor was it ever a topic of conversation or observation that I was not included with them in these amazing and professionally profitable experiences. Hmm.

I fought against transforming into a replica of the helplessly mute and apologetic face of the only other African American professional at the firm, who was also female. When the summer ended, so did my relationship with that particular firm. Although they gave me outstanding recommendations, with such a horrible experience that sickened me to my stomach and damaged my psyche, I was pretty much done with working for any law firm.

Further, as a result of that experience, I vowed to never allow myself to work for an organization where I felt "less than," or where I was disrespected or devalued — all for the sake of a paycheck. However, the highlight of that experience led me to choose my eventual career path as an employment attorney.

It became my life's work to ensure that no one else experienced what I did. So, I began to advocate for and litigate on behalf of those who felt wronged and silenced in the workplace, and to hold companies and decision-makers accountable for engaging in the unlawful and disrespectful treatment of those with whom they had an employment relationship.

It's ironic and extraordinarily frustrating to note that the toxic and hostile environment I experienced as a legal intern, probably wouldn't meet the legal definition of unlawful workplace discrimination or harassment. If I had tried to challenge the fact that I had been subjected to racial discrimination due to the firm's failure to provide me with the same terms and conditions of employment for my internship as they did for the other students who didn't look like me, not only would I have most likely lost the case, I would have also assuredly ruined my professional reputation before it even began.

As strong as my moral compass was, I was pointed in the direction that what had happened to me was not fair, and that no one deserved to be treated differently because of the color of their skin. I was passionate about doing something to correct this injustice and the idea of doing anything that would damage my nascent legal career was not an option for me. This "damned if you do, damned if you don't" dynamic is precisely what plagues so many professional women of color to this day.

Pervasiveness of Workplace Harassment

Workplace harassment remains a persistent problem, plaguing every sector (public and private) and every field of employment. Yet too often, the behavior goes unreported. Roughly, three out of four individuals who experience harassment in the workplace never talk to a supervisor or a manager about the harassing conduct. They rely mostly on sharing their experiences with family and close friends.

If the laws are there to protect individuals from harassment and discrimination in the workplace, why don't more people take advantage of the process? Quite simply, it's fear. Fear that no one will believe or care about their claim. Fear that no action will be taken to even review what has been reported, let alone punish the offender(s) for their behavior. Fear of being blamed as being responsible for inciting or causing the offensive behavior, or fear of being ostracized or otherwise subjected to social or professional retaliation for reporting the claims in the first place.

Make no mistake about it...the fear is real. Nearly 75% of employees, who actually speak out and challenge the mistreatment in their workforce, faced some form of retaliation from their employer.[xvii] This number is astounding -- especially considering that retaliating against an employee who has complained about discrimination and harassment in the workplace is also illegal.

So, what's the solution here? What can we really do to address and drive out discrimination and harassment in the workplace? Most of us are not in the position to institute meaningful change within our work environments. We don't write or enforce the Standards of Conduct or the HR policies. We don't report directly to the CEO. We are not responsible for providing training and awareness, or for holding offending employees accountable.

The sad truth that many of us know all too well that instead of reporting the mistreatment, harassment or hostile work environment and shining a light on its ugliness. Most folks endure the behavior. They avoid the harasser or attempt to downplay the gravity of the situation. They seek out advice and support from family and close friends or they simply leave the job, if they are in a position to do so.

Strategic Solutions

When faced with difficult situations, the solutions can often times be equally challenging. Since there is no proverbial magic wand that we can wave to make all the bad and negative influences in our life disappear, we have to take certain matters in our own hands. Below are a few strategies that have proven to be beneficial for others and me within personal and professional circles when we face hostile or toxic situations in the workplace.

My Advice For You...

1. Protect Yourself: Stop It! Report It! I always advocate for the most proactive solution first. If you can, address the person individually to cease the behavior. If your company has a written policy against harassment and discrimination, follow the complaint procedures within that policy. If there is no such policy, then report the behavior to your supervisor (or another member of management, if your supervisor is part of the problem). Of course, you always have the option of consulting an attorney and/or reporting your concerns to the local Equal Employment Opportunity Commission office. (Go to www.eeoc.org for more information). It just may be time to call in the law!

If you choose to take this route and pursue legal action, you could find vindication for your suffering. A court could rule in your favor, making it known that you had been subjected to unlawful discrimination and harassment. You could be awarded substantial money for damages to compensate your losses and punish the company for their wrongdoing. Or you could receive a financial settlement from your company.

However, please note, this option is not for the faint of heart and is not without risks. A legal battle with your employer could easily take years to resolve, with no guarantee of an outcome. You could spend a tremendous amount of time, money and emotional resources and end up with nothing to show for your efforts. Only you know what this fight means to you - just be sure to consider all the pros and cons.

2. Protect Yourself: Release the negativity. If reporting or complaining about the harassing behavior and/or the resulting hostile work environment is not an option (or like in my case, the behavior doesn't quite rise to the legal definition of unlawful conduct), you still need to determine who, if any, can be an ally for you in the workplace. Who can be your sounding board - someone to walk with you in the parking lot as you vent? Who can read an email for you before you send it or talk you down from the raging rafters? Find someone who will allow you - in the moment - to vent, get it out of your system, and re-direct you to the task at hand. Be mindful, this is not the time to call on the friend or colleague who is always ready for a fight and who will only escalate your anger or frustration. This is the time for cooler heads to prevail.

3. Protect Yourself: Assess the situation. As you experience those encounters that suggest you aren't being treated fairly or with respect, consider the frequency and severity of these occurrences. While you assess your working situation, consider the following:
- How often has this behavior taken place?
- How likely is it to reoccur?
- What is your company's culture for such behavior?
- Did the offender feel comfortable making the statements or behaving in such an offensive manner because others are also doing it openly? Or did they engage in the behavior more discreetly without knowledge, or approval from management?
- Does your company have a written policy against workplace discrimination, bullying and harassment, including a provision that protects against retaliation?
- Is a member of management aware of the behavior?
  - o If yes, how did they become aware?
  - o Did they personally witness or observe the behavior? Or did you or someone else report it to them?
- How seriously does your company take such complaints of harassment?

- How were others who raised concerns or complaints treated after doing so?
- Do you have a diary or journal that documents these events, as they happened? If not, start one.

Your completion of this assessment exercise will help you determine if it is worth your time, talents and energy to remain with your present employer or whether it is time to take your talents elsewhere.

4. Protect Yourself: Know your value/appreciate your worth. When the struggles of dealing with a hostile work environment weigh us down, we often began to internalize that negativity. We doubt our education, skills, abilities, and effectiveness, then it continues to go on and on. To avoid falling into this trap, it may be necessary to remind yourself of your awesomeness!! I have found it extremely helpful to speak life and positivity into myself when facing bleak and negative situations.

Perhaps there is a particular affirmation that rings true to you. If not, please get in the habit of nourishing your psyche with words that uplift, inspire and strengthen you. Say to yourself (or better yet, write it down and post it somewhere that you will see it when you need it most).

I am smart. I look great today. My natural (relaxed, braided, sewn-in) hair is beautiful and an awesome reflection of who I am today. I am educated and know this stuff backward and forward. I can do all things through Christ who strengthens me.

Whatever speaks to you, kicks you into the next gear and gets you ready for another day - use it daily, if necessary. Do not lose sight of your worth or fail to fully appreciate the value of all that you bring to the table.

5. Protect Yourself: Take a break. What are you prepared to do to ensure your physical, mental and spiritual wellbeing if you decide to remain in an environment with full knowledge that the offensive behavior is not likely to change? The repeated exposure to such negativity or a single significant event is likely to take a toll on your mind, body, and soul.

If the behavior is not addressed or remedied, in the interest of self-preservation, consider removing yourself from the situation - even if it's temporary. Consider taking a mental health day, a vacation, a "stay-cation" or, if warranted, seek guidance from a professional healthcare provider for an extended absence. Take the time you need to care for yourself.

6. Protect Yourself: Be an advocate for yourself. If you're currently in a hostile or toxic work environment, it's an individual and personal decision of whether or not you decide to stay. Whatever that decision is, be intentional and purposeful and unapologetic. Be in command of the decision. You are **NOT** a victim. You are not silenced.

Find your voice and use it to stand up for yourself! Develop an exit strategy. Even if you decide to stay, you may need it later. Don't allow anyone else to dictate your destiny or career. The choice is yours - take back your power and own your career.

Chapter 8

The World Is Getting Better For Women, One Step At A Time
By Cheryl Snapp Conner

As the CEO of a strategic communications company, SnappConner PR, I have been in the workplace for more than 30 years, since graduating from Brigham Young University in 1981.

I feel very fortunate to have never been sexually harassed by a male superior or colleague. I was very blessed that my first career position placed me under the tutelage of a very strong woman leader, who became a priceless mentor and ultimately a treasured friend until the time of her death approximately five years ago.

But this is not to say my career experience was perfect. From the earliest days of college and my choice to emphasize English as a prospective future professor, I was warned by college advisors that my universities of choice—Brigham Young University and Ricks College (now BYU Idaho), being privately-owned and church-run schools, would surely receive a minimum of "20 male applicants, who are breadwinners" for every position I could expect to emerge. "Save yourself and give up," seemed to be the message, even while I was being complimented and honored for my academic success.

This was not illegal for a private university. In the latter 70s, in fact, it was not uncommon for any organization to openly opt in favor of male employees.

I was grateful for the guidance that was meant for my own good but continued on, undeterred. I graduated in a December, eight months pregnant with my child number one. The university mailed my diploma. I had no desire to march in commencement.

From there, I had the tremendous opportunity to serve as the first live-in manager for ExtraSpace Storage, for a founder and owner who was proud to exemplify every entrepreneur, whether woman or man. It was not a high-paying role, but was a great entrepreneurial experience for me as I took that project to 100% occupancy within its first months of life.

Then came the career opportunity of a lifetime, as a young writer for an emerging technology company called Novell. Although HR policies made it difficult for my salary to progress at the speed I'd have liked, I was free to grow professionally as fast as I was able. Within 90 days I was named PR manager of the organization, directing the communications efforts of the company through four acquisitions and an IPO. My communications savvy gave me access to the highest leaders in the organization and to the company's most important accounts. I became the person executives would gravitate to when it was necessary to communicate a difficult message.

My first negative challenge arrived in the form of a stalker. An eccentric 30-something executive—one who was reportedly personally acquainted and tied to the CEO—began to show up with increasing frequency, making excuses to set meetings that I didn't believe I had the right to refuse. He began to offer "help" in the form of strategies and connections, and made it known that if my assistance was pleasing, he was in a position to "see that my career would go exceptionally well."

While he didn't make romantic overtures, the situation became increasingly "creepy"—so much so that when a requirement came up to drive to a neighboring city for an article interview, I asked my reporting supervisor to allow me to reject the offer of a ride from the executive and make the 45-minute drive on my own.

What I didn't realize until much later was that the man was exhibiting classic grooming behavior in his efforts to form an exclusive attachment to me. In one meeting, he shared his life's most vulnerable secrets, announcing that I was now "the only person in the world to know." He sent his favorite childhood photo to me. Unnerved, I dropped it into a file. Then he left a document on my chair, outlining the marketing strategy he had written that I was to enact in the company "as his personal gift."

At this point, I was frightened and alerted the Senior Vice President who was my personal mentor and boss. She was alarmed as well and instructed me to cut off all contact with the individual and to let her know if he attempted anything more.

He began sending emails—expressing admiration at first, but increasingly angry and threatening as I refused to respond. (I should note here that these were the earliest days of corporate email, before it was commonly understood that emails are company property and subject to company and HR review.) I gave the emails to my boss. She reported the harassment to both HR and to the police, who issued a restraining order.

With his emails as evidence, the company's HR department fired the man. While I should have been entirely relieved, I was mortified at the office drama I imagined I had created in some way, over an issue I didn't want to be associated with in any respect. I feared that I had let down the CEO, who had given this person a job despite his eccentricities as a gesture of help. I felt like a naïve child, wondering how I had missed the signals, what I should have done and when I should have done it.

Worst of all, my former husband—a domineering man who had resented my career success from the start—worked at the same technology company. Without my knowledge, he went to the HR department to confirm for himself the facts of the firing and to ascertain whether I had welcomed or been "asking for" the man's attention in any way, which horrified me even more than the actual stalking abuse.

In hindsight, I am exceedingly grateful for a responsive company and boss who supported me in exactly the way I would have hoped. For others, I would like to see every individual, both woman and man, be educated about the grooming behaviors that signal a cause for alarm, and learn what to do to protect their personal and professional boundaries in a situation like this.

In the years that followed the stalking, my career was thankfully unaffected. I heard through business associates the man had obtained several other positions that ended in similar ways. Eventually, he reached out to me directly and apologized for his actions, asking if I could forgive him and maintaining that he had only wanted (and desperately wanted) to be considered a friend. I accepted his apology and told him all was forgiven and that he could move on in peace, but that too much water had passed under the bridge to be friends (although I no longer held any fears that he would be a danger to me).

The worst outcome, however, was that my former husband, despite all reassurances from the company and from even my boss—deemed the situation to have been entirely my fault. In his estimation, it had been an "emotional affair" that I had "asked for" and that he considered to be a wrong so great that I could not be forgiven. In my eventual divorce, he brought the situation up again, now blown up as an office "affair" heinous enough to justify his mistreatment of me for all of the 17 years afterward until our divorce.

I was chagrined but not deterred by the giant stories. But it was interesting to note that while my company and employer were blessedly supportive in this situation, the biggest injury for me was the personal cost. Had I been better educated on how to handle a situation like this, I could have cut it off at the pass. As for the marriage, however, the blown up story was perhaps one more sign of an unrecoverable situation. Had this story not occurred, I am certain that another would have emerged in its place.

Career Lessons Learned

As the stalker issue was resolved, I faced my next situation in the form of an authoritative vice president (a male) who favored hierarchical management and who resented the favored access I had. In the reporting structure, he fell between me and the Senior Vice President who'd been mentoring me.

To assert his authority, he made my life very hard. Assignments submitted on a Wednesday would land in his inbox and be purposely disregarded until Friday p.m. On one such occasion he ordered me at 5:00 on a Friday evening to follow him into the conference room for a thorough review of my slides. (This was in the day of actual slides in a tray, as PowerPoint had not yet come to be.)

He put his finger on a bulleted slide, then instructed me to advance to the next. Did the bullet on the next frame land in the exact position? No? Re-do! With a flourish, he dropped the tray back into my hands with orders that they be re-done and that I be in New York with a new final by Monday a.m., despite the fact that every slide maker within a 100-mile radius had already been tied up with similar demands.

With my three young children, no help from my spouse and no babysitter available in the late hours of the night, I found a slide creator from another department, promised to pay for his overtime, and proceeded to meet him in the evening with my children in tow. I knew how unfair it was, but like the stalker situation, it didn't occur to me there was anyone I would dare to talk to about a situation like this.

I mutely complied with the demands while muttering under my breath. Nearing the end of my rope, I began to make plans for a freelance career. If I were my own boss, I reasoned, I would not be working late hours unless they were by my own choice, when my children were sleeping, and only for situations that were legitimately required. I could provide my services back to this company (and others) and could be paid a fair price for the work they received.

I completed my plan, feeling it was the only way I could responsibly work while taking appropriate care of my children. Fighting back tears, I shored up the courage to give my notice and make my employer aware of my plans.

In the conversation that followed, I received the surprise of my life. While I had been too scared to come forward, unbeknownst to me, the VP's overbearing and unprofessional behavior was known. He was being let go, and I was being considered as his replacement. Had I been proactive when the behavior started, this might have been the career possibility of a lifetime. But instead, as I struggled to bear my burdens in silence, I had become incredibly burned out. My emotions had turned another direction and I was actually very excited about the prospect of beginning a consulting career of my own.

Again, destiny had worked in my favor. In spite of the reason for my leap away from corporate life, entrepreneurship has proven to be an ideal path for me. In my new role, my income immediately tripled. In the consulting arena there is far less worry or care whether the provider is a woman or man.

Your Reputation Is Your Gold

For all of us, it is vital to be a visible and known example of the principles we believe. We need to be "on the record"—not only in the press, but in all of our actions, for being the kind of people we aspire and proclaim to be. "How you do anything is how you do everything," the motto goes. We should strive to be our best selves, not only in public, but during the times that no one is looking and no one is likely to know.

Character, authenticity, resilience and the courage to act are our protections, even beyond the protection of HR policy or the law. These are the things we should remember in becoming all that we are able to be, and in moving our legacy forward for others as well.

My Advice For You...

1. In the midst of a bad situation, do not make assumptions. You should never endure a bad situation in helpless silence or make a career decision that is centered on fear. Your greatest opportunities will come from your ability to step up in a productive way with appropriate proposals to move a situation forward—not from enduring in silence until somebody else observes a problem and is forced to intervene from above.

2. Entrepreneurship is power. Clients who are seeking good service are willing to pay for results. This is an arena where women executives who are naturally inclined to seek synergies and collaborative outcomes can shine.

3. Management is a skill and a challenge—learn it well. In the role of a company leader, I have learned many lessons. In two cases (one with a woman partner and one with a man) I found myself partnered with individuals whose agenda was ultimately to be the "person in charge" and to relegate me, as a less aggressive personality, to a role of perpetual client service and billable hours. While it was not easy, I extracted myself from both of these limiting opportunities.

At the helm of my own business, however, I have also encountered the challenges of being a CEO. In this case, I learned that the first people to join, regardless of their desires for joining, were not destined to be the best people to assist in our growth. I found myself working longer hours than ever to support the expectations of individuals who didn't take my leadership seriously, believing that because they were first in, they could never be fired. And in truth, I didn't fire them—both eventually broke non-compete (which was understood to be binding but not yet ratified in a legal contract) to join a competitor. While the initial discovery of the betrayals was painful, ultimately, I was relieved they were gone and am managing our current organization in a much better way.

4. Your future is what you make it. At the end of the day - and particularly in the Freedom Economy that encourages and rewards freelance business—our futures, as women and men, is what we make of them. My words of advice to younger professionals is to be productive, but in doing so, be proactive in providing all the value you can and to receive in exchange every bit of the value you are worth. If a situation is not working, it is your opportunity and responsibility to change it.

Changing positions and even changing careers is not a negative thing, although a wise professional will do all within their power to sustain and protect their working partnerships and to move forward when needed without burning bridges.

5. The partnerships you create are your gold. One wise executive—a man who has served at the helm of companies ranging from startups to Fortune 500—noted that he rose quickly and effortlessly throughout his career with little thought to the impact of his rise on the others around him. Years later, to divert attention from sagging revenue in a downturn, two of the board members for the company he worked for unfairly accused the man of wrongdoing. They spurred an SEC investigation (that was covered by the press) and had him publicly fired.

To the man's regret, he suddenly realized that in the years of his rise, he had neglected to forge the partnerships that might have helped him turn this situation around. "There was nobody who had my back," he recalls. Remember to help others along your way, not only because it's the right thing to do, but because the day will come that your willingness to help others will influence their willingness to help you, too, in a time of need that you could have never predicted.

Chapter 9

Become The Master Of Your Fate
By Christy Rutherford

So, there you have it. Powerful, traumatic, dramatic and heart-breaking stories from seven incredibly courageous women who didn't let life break them. The difference between a CHAMPION and a loser is a Champion keeps getting back up after life knocks them down. This is a small snapshot into the lives of these ladies, so you can imagine what the rest of our careers looked like.

For most of the ladies, this is their first time EVER sharing these stories publicly. **CHAMPIONS NEVER TELL!** They never told their stories because they didn't want to be perceived as weak or in a negative light, but as you can see they are strong and powerful.

It takes a lot to lay your heart open and be vulnerable to the criticisms and judgment of others, but they did it to stop millions of women around the world from suffering. That's a different level of leadership and I'm so grateful they agreed to share their stories to motivate you to choose a different path for your life.

When Leadership Protects You

Reflecting on Cheryl's story of when she told her supervisors about the harassment and they took swift and appropriate action, it built trust with her that she mattered. It also demonstrated her organizations' commitment to not tolerating harassment. Like Cheryl, I'm fortunate to not have been sexually harassed during my career. However, there were times as a leader where I was able to intervene in situations like her supervisor.

Nearly 12 years ago, one of my young leaders came to me with tears in her eyes. She said while inspecting offices the previous night, the male that she accompanied made her extremely uncomfortable. Having a reputation for open and honest conversation with my direct reports and protecting them, I asked her to tell me exactly what happened. She confessed that when they opened the door to a room with a bed in it, he said that he should throw her on the bed and have his way with her.

I can't really remember what I did....but we never saw him again. She had no reason to fabricate a story and there was no reason for me not to believe her, so the situation was handled. I share this story because when I asked her about that incident earlier this year, she didn't remember it happening. I asked if she was serious and she really couldn't remember. I couldn't believe it! How could she forget something that rocked her world for that brief moment?

I'll tell you why, and this is what I know for sure, it's because it was handled swiftly. She wasn't asked to give a written or verbal statement and relive the incident over and over again through mounds of bureaucratic paperwork. She didn't have to stand in front of a room and try to convince other men that what she said was true. She didn't have to walk with him repeatedly and be afraid every time they came upon that room. She didn't have to see him daily and smile while her skin crawled from his disgusting comment.

She NEVER saw him again and therefore, the memory of something that could have turned into a scar, became a non-issue and she's flourished into an amazing senior leader in the organization.

It's up to leaders and organizations to hold others accountable for their actions, regardless of their position and value. Everyone is replaceable, and when leaders allow tyrants, harassers, and people that lack moral character to flourish and not be held accountable, it erodes the morale of the organization and permeates the culture. This has significant impact on engagement, loyalty, and retention.

Organizations spend billions of dollars to train their personnel on these three pillars, but fail to address people who operate outside of good moral standard, which makes the investment in training fruitless.

When Leadership Fails You

The stories in this book highlight that other people witness the harassment and don't anything. The tyrants and bullies had widespread reputations, but the organization chose to keep them, even as they bullied and harassed others.

This is identical to Harvey Weinstein and the Uber CEO. People knew. They saw it. They witnessed it…but no one took action until many people's lives had been impacted negatively.

When you think about how your organization is set up, is it set up for you to be effective? What are the steps that you can go through to protect yourself and your organization? Is your organization set up to protect you from being harassed? And if it's not, *what are you going to do about it?* That's a true question.

A number of people think a minority or woman issue is somebody else's problem. They point fingers and say, "That's HR's problem."

"That's the civil rights person's problem."

"That's the diversity and inclusion problem."

"No, that's the leader's problem."

At the end of the day, IT'S YOUR PROBLEM.

It is your problem because you're not doing anything to change the circumstance. What will you do differently? Are you going to stay and complain every day? Are you going to stay and have your body riddled with disease? Are you going to stay and end up having PTSD?

It's time for you make the decision to do something different. There are organizations who want you and will value your talent. I don't want to keep telling people to leave, but if it gets down to whether or not you're going to die, or whether or not you're going to have PTSD, or whether or not you're going to have zero self-confidence, just to say that you still have a title and some money, it's time to go!

There Is A Better Way

You deserve to live a life of total fulfillment. You deserve peace, joy, happiness, love and financial security. However, if you're caught in the negative cycle at work, it's hard to picture a great life if you're in the fire.

There is a significant increase in the number of professional women who suffer from depression, whether they know it or not. Depression is another label that ambitious women are not willing to carry, so it can go unrecognized and untreated. You don't have to take medication if you're depressed, but you have to do SOMETHING! Whether it's leaving work early to do things that you love, getting a pet, taking yoga, meditating or dancing to Madonna and Beyonce daily, you have to do something to break the negative cycle of energy.

If you are mitigating your stress and anxiety with medication or wine nightly because you feel trapped in your job, how is it making you better? Don't settle for where you are. The world is waiting for your greatness! Give yourself permission to shift from your job and move into your purpose and live a life of significance, not just one with a high-power title.

Work on forgiving others and letting go of the past pain. If you've finally achieved the position you worked so hard for, but it doesn't feel like a victory because of the challenges you experienced, what's the point? If you feel the pain of gaining high levels of success more than the joy of achieving it, learn to celebrate where you are, and let go of what it took to get there.

Instead of succumbing to Golden Handcuffs, create a Plan B. Consider downsizing your lifestyle and reinvesting your money. Stacking your money will give you so much more security than any job can provide. What side business can you run in your free time or on the weekends that will generate additional income? What hobbies do you have to create products to sell at the farmer's market or on Etsy? You don't need a million dollars to start a business. Start where you are with what you have.

Lastly, start networking with other successful women in your industry and city/town. Join a local group and attend monthly gatherings to expand your professional network. People are always looking for great people to fill positions. How will they find you if you're always at work, on the phone for hours complaining about your job or drinking at home on the couch?

Begin to work AT ONCE on your Plan B and create a path to shift you out of the job that is sucking the life out of you.

Bear Hugs Kettle

Emmet Fox tells a story in, *Around the Year*, called Bear Hugs Kettle. He says a bear goes around a campfire and sees a kettle. The kettle is on the fire and it's warm. The bear hugs the kettle and it creates comfort for him and gives him security because it's cold outside. After some time, the kettle starts to burn the bear, but he hugs it tighter because it's something that once gave him comfort and security. He's confused and no matter how much it burns, he won't let go. Therefore, the bear hugs the kettle to his demise and dies.

Is your job the kettle? Is your job something that once gave you security and comfort, but is creating your demise? If you are holding onto something that is killing you, it's time to let it go. If you're holding onto something that is creating medical conditions within you, it's time to let it go. If you are beaten down to a pulp where you no longer recognize yourself in the mirror and you can't remember how great you are, it doesn't matter, run away.

Sisterhood – Loving One Another

The only way we're going to get more women in the executive levels is we have to do the work to put them there. We have to be the mentors, sponsors and host the events to get women to the higher levels. This includes ALL Women, and it's especially important for women of color.

Women, in general, have a looooong way to go and the only way we are going to arrive at our destination to create a better world for the next generation of women is to work together to make things happen for us.

Mentoring young women and ensuring they are armed for challenges early in their careers. That's how we can contribute to getting a large number of qualified women in the pipeline for executive-level leadership. We may just have to do it ourselves. The women that I mentored will far surpass anything that I accomplished and that's the way it should be.

What can you do to serve the ladies in your office or industry? But first! What are you doing to save yourself? The greatest challenge we have in saving others is how are we going to save other women if we're drowning?

Do the work in this book. Take the advice and offerings from the ladies in this book. Go through the process and do what's necessary to save yourself, so you can in turn, save others!

About The Authors
Jil Jordan Greene

Jil Jordan Greene is CEO of The People Resource Group, a Change Management, HR Consulting, Leadership & Development Firm. We provide HR services, business strategies, and solutions that help organizations accelerate their growth and increase their bottom line.

She is an expert when it comes to Team Building and Company Retreats for small businesses, nonprofit organizations and professional service firms. Her clients describe her as "the Surgeon" because she operates on their company's culture with precision.

Greene gained her 15-year HR expertise in corporate America working for some of the country's top Fortune 500 companies in the restaurant, hospitality, and entertainment industries, in roles ranging from Recruiter, Vice president of Human Resources, and Chief People Officer.

She has been recognized in her industry by receiving the Most Powerful and Influential Women of Louisiana Award, a Woman of the Year Nominee Award, and Workforce Magazine's Game Changer Award, and The Top 20 People to Know in HR.

Jil is also an author, radio host, and national keynote speaker.

Christy Rutherford

Christy Rutherford is the President of LIVE-UP Leadership. She's an executive leadership coach, trainer, keynote speaker and best-selling author. Christy published five #1 best-selling books on Amazon in 8 months.

A Harvard Business School Alumna from the Program for Leadership Development, Christy also earned a degree in Agricultural Business from South Carolina State University, an MBA from Averett University, a Diploma Sous Chef de Patisserie from Alain and Marie Lenotre Culinary Institute, and an Executive Leadership Coaching Certification from Georgetown University.

Christy served over 16 years as an active duty military officer and is the 13th African American woman to achieve the rank of Commander in the organization's 225+ year history.

Her tours expanded from drug interdictions on the high seas; emergency response to hundreds of maritime accidents/oil spills; responding to the needs of the citizens in New Orleans two days after Hurricane Katrina; and a Congressional Fellowship with the House of Representatives.

Among her many professional accomplishments, her national recognition includes Cambridge Who's Who Amongst Executives and Professionals, Career Communications STEM Technology All-Star and the Edward R. Williams Award for Excellence In Diversity.

Join her community: **www.wlmwc.com**
Website: **www.christyrutherford.com**

Cheryl Snapp Conner

Cheryl Snapp Conner is founder and CEO of SnappConner PR and creator of Content University™. She is a popular speaker, author and national columnist on business communication and PR. In 2014, ClearPoint Strategies named her one of the world's Top 20 Business Thought Leaders to Follow.

Since the launch of SnappConner PR in April 2007, the agency has established itself as a top US thought leadership and communications firm, winning Top Tech Communicator recognition and multiple awards for agency growth. Cheryl has been named to Signal Peak's v100 list each year since 2008. She has been recognized by Utah Business Magazine's *30 Women to Watch* and is a two-time finalist in the Utah Women in Technology awards. Prior to forming her first agency in 1989, Snapp Conner was Director of Public Relations for Novell.

Conner is a popular contributor to the Entrepreneurs channel for *Forbes* and a guest contributor to *WSJ Startups*.

Dr. Valorie Parker-Hagan

Businesswoman, Author, Radio Personality, Life Coach & Speaker, Dr. Valorie N. Parker-Hagan is the President and CEO of Arise by VNP and Associates, INC., a Speaker's Bureau & Public Relations Company. She went from making $35,000 a year in small jobs, to a 6 figure income as the primary booking agent for Les Brown Enterprises and Les Brown Speaker's Network as well as Speakers Nationally.

Dr. Valorie is the founder of The Soul of a Woman Foundation, Inc., which was developed to raise awareness of the needs of women and children living in abusive homes, providing housing, financial assistance, career development, and other urban and social justice issues facing local and national communities.

Representing international speakers for the past 18 years, she's also a captivating speaker in her own right. She shares insight about her painful 19-year abusive marriage, turning events into powerful experiences, allowing her to encourage and enrich the lives of everyone she encounters.

A national and international radio show host, Valorie has been hosting "Hot Topics From The Soul" for eight years. Dr. Valorie developed the Soul of the Woman series which includes a CD, *From Pain to Power*.

An author of four books, she's published *From The Soul Of A Woman, Love Shouldn't Hurt; Unveiling Secrets From The Heart, Forgiving Your Past To Free Your Future; Restored Vessels, Young*

Adults Overcoming Adversity; and her latest release, *Unlimited Possibilities.*

Her Accomplishments also include:
•Ph.D. in Social Work Services from ELST School of Ministry-April 2012
•Certified Life Coach July 2010
•Certificate of Honor from Set @ Liberty, Weapons of Purpose Summit 2010
•Board Member Lauderhill Regional Chamber of Commerce 2009-2011
•Founded Hot Topics from The Soul Talk Show Jan 2009
•Power Networking Facilitator/George Fraser 2008
•Member of Grace, Mercy & Peace Empowerment Group 2008
•Awarded Keys to The City of Norfolk VA-by Zo El Ministries 2008
•Member TWEF (Texas Woman Empowerment Foundation) 2008
•Who's Who in Black South Florida 2007
•Founded the Soul of a Woman Foundation 2007
•Awarded Exemplary Service Award by Channel 3 Elect Lady 2006
•Member Faith Center Ministries 2003-Present
•Founded Les Brown's Platinum Program 2003
•Promoter for Les Brown's 1st Family of Motivation Tour 2002
•Founded Arise By VNP 2001

Jade Brown Russell

Jade Brown Russell, is a proud native of New Orleans. She is Principal of JD Russell Consulting, LLC, a full service firm focusing on regulatory compliance, legal counsel, business solutions, governmental relations and strategic planning. Jade is the former regional general counsel of operations at Caesars Entertainment, where she addressed litigation, gaming, corporate and regulatory and compliance issues for the company's properties in Louisiana, Biloxi, MS and Ohio. She is a co-founder and former partner at Transcendent Legal, and former Executive Director of the French Market Corporation.

Since her return to New Orleans, Jade has become civically involved in several organizations. She currently serves as a Director and Past Chairman of the Downtown Development District. She also serves as Vice Chair of the Urban League of Louisiana. She is also a founding member and former President of the Urban League of Greater New Orleans Young Professionals.

Jade also serves on the board of directors for the Arts Council of New Orleans, Ashe Cultural Center, and Bricolage Academy. In 2013 and 2008, Jade was honored as a New Orleans City Business Woman of the Year, and in 2009 and 2011, she received the Urban League's Rising Star Award for her professional and civic accomplishments. Jade has been named to both Orleans Parish D.A. Leon Cannizzaro's and New Orleans Mayor Mitch Landrieu's transition teams, and most recently was appointed Chair of the Mayor's Tricentennial Community Engagement Committee.

A Howard University and Southern University Law Center graduate, Jade has a sincere passion for mentorship. Jade continues to create and cultivate opportunities for African American women by building a pipeline for mentorship and sharing life and career strategies with women and girls of all ages. Jade is the proud mother of 11 year-old, Jadon and 5 year-old, Dorsett

Ronetta J. Francis

Ronetta J. Francis is a seasoned employment attorney, with over 23 years combined practicing as a senior trial attorney with the federal government for the Fourth Circuit Court of Appeals and the U.S. Equal Employment Opportunity Commission, and as in-house counsel for Walmart Stores, Inc. She bridged her legal background with business acumen, leading the employment compliance and ethics functions for Walmart, as the Vice President of US Ethics and Employment Compliance.

Ronetta is a motivational speaker and leadership coach, she has parlayed her Bloom Where You're Planted philosophy in to actionable strategies to perceive and achieve the pathways toward successful results.

Ronetta is an active member of Alpha Kappa Alpha Sorority, Inc. for more than 28 years, having held various leadership roles. Her community involvement also supports many local organizations, such as the Samaritan Center, the Northwest Arkansas Women's Shelter, as well as the National Alliance on Mental Illness and the Alzheimer's Association on a national level. Ronetta and her husband, Earl C. Francis, Jr., have been married for 24 years, and have three adult daughters, Erica, Jordan, and Dana.

VonGretchen Nelson

VonGretchen C. Nelson is a Diversity and Inclusion Strategist, Educator, Talent Advisor, Entrepreneur and Engaging Public Speaker. She is passionate about securing a more inclusive global workforce for generations to come through training, education, and awareness. She received her M.A. in Human Resource Management with a concentration in Organizational Management from Walden University. She holds a B.S. in Family and Consumer Sciences with a concentration in Child Development from South Carolina State University.

VonGretchen was recently named President and CEO of PCC Global Institute, LLC. PCCGI brings awareness through in-person and online training and professional development. The website (**www.pccgius.com**), is a resource for Workplace Diversity & Inclusion Training, ERG Development & Execution, Professional & Team Building Development, D&I Consulting and Strategy Services.

In addition to her leadership role at PCCGI, VonGretchen also serves as Vice President of Diversity and Inclusion for AGI (Aperion Global Institute). In addition to VonGretchen corporate experience, she has held the position of President for a local non-profit, People, Community and Culture for over ten years. The South Carolina based non-profit focuses on assisting the unemployed and underemployed life skills such as: interviewing, professionalism in the workplace, personal branding, personalized elevate speech, parenting skills, and financial literacy.

VonGretchen has received numerous awards and recognition for her contributions within the Diversity & Inclusion field by numerous corporations, organizations and colleges/universities. She has reached over 10,000 students over the past 10 years assisting with job placement, resume, cover letter writing and/or behavioral based interview techniques.

Special Thanks To Johnny Mack
For your consulting and oversight of this amazing project.

SPAN: Self Published Authors Network
www.SPANbooks.com

info@SPANbooks.com

Special Thanks To Michelle Washington
For your support and designing the cover

Women of MORE Magazine
www.womenofmore.com

Special Thanks To Sonia Jackson
For your support and willingness to share your testimonial

Sonia Jackson Myles is . . .
Designing Her Destiny
& Helping Others
Do The Same!

Sonia Jackson Myles, Founder & CEO of The Sister
Accord LLC and The Accord Group LLC.
Author, NAACP Image Award Nominated Book,
The Sister Accord: 51 Ways To LOVE Your Sister.

Special Thanks To Bennie Randall
For your support and willingness to share your testimonial

A Private Community For Entrepreneurs and
Small Business Startups

www.BennieOnDemand.com

APPENDIX

Day 1 Check-In
Date - _____

1. On a scale from 1-5 (1-poor – 5-great) how would you consider your:

Overall Health	1	2	3	4	5
Work-Life Balance	1	2	3	4	5
Stress Level	1	2	3	4	5
Relationships with family	1	2	3	4	5
Relationships with friends	1	2	3	4	5
Overall satisfaction with life	1	2	3	4	5
Time Management	1	2	3	4	5

2. What are the 3 top priorities you would like to resolve this quarter? (Dates_____)
a.
b.
c.

3. On average, how many hours of sleep do you get a night?___

4. What's the quality of your sleep? Poor   Good   Great

5. On a scale from 1-5 (1-not really – 5-Absolutely!) you'd like to be more:

Spiritual	1	2	3	4	5
Grateful	1	2	3	4	5
Happier	1	2	3	4	5
Disciplined	1	2	3	4	5
Personally Developed	1	2	3	4	5
Grounded In Truth	1	2	3	4	5
Clean In Your Heart	1	2	3	4	5
Optimistic	1	2	3	4	5

6. What can you do differently?

31 Days To Mental, Physical and Spiritual Health

Day 1 - Meditate for 5 minutes. Find a meditative app or go to YouTube and search guided meditations, aum chanting or singing bowls. Whichever works best for you. Start with one day a week, before important meetings or when you feel like you're melting down.

Date										
Done										

Day 2 – Turn your car or commute into a personal development university. Turnoff the radio and download some books or listen to something that addresses a challenge you're having today.

A few of my favorite books: *Outwitting The Devil* by Napoleon Hill .ANYTHING from Napoleon Hill!. *Think and Grow Rich For Women* by Sharon Lechter. *How to Win Friends and Influence People* by Dale Carnegie. *Forgiveness* by Iyanla Vanzant *Destiny* by T.D. Jakes.

Date										
Done										

Day 3 - Exercise at least 3 times a week. Make an effort to work out. Zumba, running and yoga are all great choices to get rid of negative energy. Workout before you leave home in the morning, at lunch or before going home. MAKE TIME if you feel you don't have it. It will save your life.

Date										
Done										

Day 4 - Write down 5 things you'd like to do or how you want to see yourself, starting with I AM. I AM healthy, I AM happy, I AM whole, I AM at peace, I AM loved. Whatever you desire. Write them down and look at yourself in the mirror and repeat the five affirmations three times.

Date											
Done											

Day 5 - Spend the first 30 minutes of your day in quiet time. Read the Bible, pray or something positive. Visualize a happier and healthier life. What do you want your life to look like? Visit your future and come back to make it a reality.

Date											
Done											

Day 6 - Walk - Go for a 30-minute walk, without music or cell phone distractions, at least 3 times a week. Take a break from your desk and go for a walk outside. Even if it's cold. Walk in the halls.

Date											
Done											

Day 7 - Forgive someone. What bag do you need to let go of? What weight are you carrying that's stopping you from living the life you desire. It's time to let it and THEM go.

Date											
Done											

Day 8 - Schedule your massage for the month or call and get one today. Make sure you get one to work the kinks out of your shoulders and back. Switch them up and get a hot stone massage. Your life will never be the same.

Date										
Done										

Day 9 - Dance to your favorite childhood song. You can never go wrong with Michael Jackson, Madonna or Prince....or Beyonce depending on your age. Dance until you feel like your old self. Even if you have to dance until you pass out.

Date										
Done										

Day 10 - Take inventory of your circle. Who are the people you need to delete from your life? Write their name down. After that, call one of your great friends and tell them how much you appreciate them. Positive conversation only – Max 5 minutes.

Date										
Done										
Delete										
Keep										

Day 11 - Set 2 goals you'd like to accomplish this month. Write them on a 3x5 notecard and put them in your office and/or bathroom mirror. Each month, place in the box below if 0, 1 or 2 were accomplished.

Date										
Done										
Number										

Day 12 - Find someone to be good to. Take someone's cart back to the store, buy a co-worker coffee or lunch, hold the door open for someone. Get some positive Karma working in your life.

Date											
Done											

Day 13 – Notice who makes you angry, upset or has negative vibes. Write down their names and avoid them. Take note of how you feel.

Date											
Done											
Name											

Day 14 – Meditate for 5 minutes.

Date											
Done											

Day 15 - Take inventory of your accomplishments. On a separate piece of paper, write down what you've accomplished in your life. Then, go to bathroom in your home or office and look yourself right in the eyes and say, I'm FREAKING AWESOME!

Date											
Done											

Day 16 – Join a professional women's network that meets monthly. Mark in the 3rd column if you actually did it and the date of the meeting you attended. If you didn't join or attend, note that too.

Date											
Done											
Meet?											

Day 17 - In the phenomenal book Pyscho-Cybernetics by Dr. Matthew Maltz, he gives <u>5 Steps for Reprogramming</u> the voice. Observing your inner voice, when it says something negative, do the following (CRAFT):
1. Cancel – say it aloud
2. Replace – with positive data
3. Affirm – the new image you desire
4. Focus – 10 mins daily
5. Train – yourself for lasting change

Date												
Done												

Day 17 - Please repeat the following statements that pertain to you aloud and internalize them if they are things you really want. Pause….and observe what the voice says to you. If it gets negative, practice the CRAFT method above.
1. I want to make more money.
2. I want a better job.
3. I want to be happier.
4. I want to be healthier.
5. I want better relationships with my family and friends.

Date												
Done												

Day 18 – Take a treat for your office colleagues. Whether it's doughnuts, fruit, cake, granola, coffee or bagels. Find a way to make others happy and you in turn will be happier. Karma

Date												
Done												

Day 19 – Laugh 10 times today. Find a reason….

Date												
Done												

Day 20 – The Law of Attraction states, whatever you focus on expands. What do you find yourself thinking about and talking about most of the time? All negative things and drama? Is it any wonder that's all you get? Catch yourself thinking and saying negative things and say positive things only. Go back to your affirmations from earlier in the month.

Date											
Done											

Day 21 - Learn the art of saying "No." If someone asks you to do something you don't want to do, do you cringe and then agree? It's time to only do things that will get you to happiness. Start to say no to things that will waste your time and make you unhappy, just to make others happy.

Date											
Done											

Day 22 – Listen to The Strangest Secret by Earl Nightengale. It's on ITunes and YouTube.

Date											
Done											

Day 23 - Emmet Fox said, "To interfere mentally in any situation involves you in the consequence just as much as would a physical interference." Become mindful of the conversations you're having on social media or in the office. Are you in someone else's business, when you need to be using that time to solve your own issues?

Date											
Done											

Day 24 – Without a vision people perish. Create a 5 year plan for your personal life. What do you want your PERSONAL life to look like in the next 5 years? Family, relationships, health, peace, joy. You should be able to see the movie of your life playing in your head. Write it down and each month, revisit it and make sure you can FEEL who you desire to be.

Date											
Done											

Day 25 - Create a 5 year plan for your professional life. What do you need to be successful PROFESSIONALLY? Will you move up in your organization or move out? What certifications do you need? What side business do you need to create to bridge the income? Write it down and create a plan to get there.

Date											
Done											

Day 26 – Take a 7 day mental diet from the news and negative information. Instead, listen to an audiobook or positive video. It's time to detox your mind, heart and body from the negativity of the world. Take 7 days off and see how you feel after that. Your life will never be the same.

Date											
Done											

Day 27 - Commit to healthy eating. What can you do to eat healthier? Take your lunch or healthy snacks to work? Actually make time to eat? Think about what you can do this month to nourish your body with the foods you eat.

Date											
Done											

Day 28 – Like Jade mentioned earlier, your squad will be the ones who know that even an anchor needs to be checked on and cared for sometimes. Call or send a note to your squad to check on them, or call them and allow them to be there for you. Make a lunch or dinner date to check in on each other.

Date											
Done											

Day 29 – Jade also mentioned, "Steve Jobs once said that you can't connect the dots looking forward – you can only connect the dots looking back." Take 10 minutes to reflect on some of the decisions that you've make in your life that have gotten you to where you are. The good and the bad ones. What can you adjust to make it greater?

Date											
Done											

Day 30 - Ask yourself: What would you do every day if all of your lifestyle expenses were paid? What problem do you want to solve for the world? Seek a job or mission within those areas and it will bring you immense joy and freedom. This is about DESTINY! What dreams are stirring around in you that need to be unleashed?

Date											
Done											

Day 31 - Joyce Meyer said, "Half of the stress that we go through is trying to pay for and take care of what we own." What can you cut back on this month to stack your money and create your break in case of emergency fund? Eating out, clothes, cell phone, downsize car? Make a plan to stack your money and it will give you greater security than any job can ever offer you.

Date											
Done											

Day 90 Check-In
Date - _____

1. On a scale from 1-5 (1-poor – 5-great) how would you consider your:

Overall Health	1	2	3	4	5
Work-Life Balance	1	2	3	4	5
Stress Level	1	2	3	4	5
Relationships with family	1	2	3	4	5
Relationships with friends	1	2	3	4	5
Overall satisfaction with life	1	2	3	4	5
Time Management	1	2	3	4	5

2. What are the 3 top priorities you would like to resolve this quarter? (Dates_____)
a.
b.
c.

3. On average, how many hours of sleep do you get a night?___

4. What's the quality of your sleep? Poor   Good   Great

5. On a scale from 1-5 (1-not really – 5-Absolutely!) you'd like to be more:

Spiritual	1	2	3	4	5
Grateful	1	2	3	4	5
Happier	1	2	3	4	5
Disciplined	1	2	3	4	5
Personally Developed	1	2	3	4	5
Grounded In Truth	1	2	3	4	5
Clean In Your Heart	1	2	3	4	5
Optimistic	1	2	3	4	5

6. What can you do differently?

Day 180 Check-In
Date - _____

1. On a scale from 1-5 (1-poor – 5-great) how would you consider your:

Overall Health	1	2	3	4	5
Work-Life Balance	1	2	3	4	5
Stress Level	1	2	3	4	5
Relationships with family	1	2	3	4	5
Relationships with friends	1	2	3	4	5
Overall satisfaction with life	1	2	3	4	5
Time Management	1	2	3	4	5

2. What are the 3 top priorities you would like to resolve this quarter? (Dates_____)
a.
b.
c.

3. On average, how many hours of sleep do you get a night?___

4. What's the quality of your sleep? Poor   Good   Great

5. On a scale from 1-5 (1-not really – 5-Absolutely!) you'd like to be more:

Spiritual	1	2	3	4	5
Grateful	1	2	3	4	5
Happier	1	2	3	4	5
Disciplined	1	2	3	4	5
Personally Developed	1	2	3	4	5
Grounded In Truth	1	2	3	4	5
Clean In Your Heart	1	2	3	4	5
Optimistic	1	2	3	4	5

6. What can you do differently?

Day 270 Check-In
Date - _____

1. On a scale from 1-5 (1-poor – 5-great) how would you consider your:

Overall Health	1	2	3	4	5
Work-Life Balance	1	2	3	4	5
Stress Level	1	2	3	4	5
Relationships with family	1	2	3	4	5
Relationships with friends	1	2	3	4	5
Overall satisfaction with life	1	2	3	4	5
Time Management	1	2	3	4	5

2. What are the 3 top priorities you would like to resolve this quarter? (Dates_____)
a.
b.
c.

3. On average, how many hours of sleep do you get a night?___

4. What's the quality of your sleep? Poor   Good   Great

5. On a scale from 1-5 (1-not really – 5-Absolutely!) you'd like to be more:

Spiritual	1	2	3	4	5
Grateful	1	2	3	4	5
Happier	1	2	3	4	5
Disciplined	1	2	3	4	5
Personally Developed	1	2	3	4	5
Grounded In Truth	1	2	3	4	5
Clean In Your Heart	1	2	3	4	5
Optimistic	1	2	3	4	5

6. What can you do differently?

Day 365 Check-In
Date - _____

1. On a scale from 1-5 (1-poor – 5-great) how would you consider your:

Overall Health	1	2	3	4	5
Work-Life Balance	1	2	3	4	5
Stress Level	1	2	3	4	5
Relationships with family	1	2	3	4	5
Relationships with friends	1	2	3	4	5
Overall satisfaction with life	1	2	3	4	5
Time Management	1	2	3	4	5

2. What are the 3 top priorities you would like to resolve this quarter? (Dates_____)
a.
b.
c.

3. On average, how many hours of sleep do you get a night?___

4. What's the quality of your sleep? Poor   Good   Great

5. On a scale from 1-5 (1-not really – 5-Absolutely!) you'd like to be more:

Spiritual	1	2	3	4	5
Grateful	1	2	3	4	5
Happier	1	2	3	4	5
Disciplined	1	2	3	4	5
Personally Developed	1	2	3	4	5
Grounded In Truth	1	2	3	4	5
Clean In Your Heart	1	2	3	4	5
Optimistic	1	2	3	4	5

6. What can you do differently?

References

[i] Ely, R., & Ibarra, H., Kolb, D. "Women Rising: The Unseen Barriers." *Harvard Business School Publishing* (2013): n. pag. Web. 15 March 2016.
[ii] Fortune Editors. (2017, June 7) "These Are The Women CEOs Leading Fortune 500 Companies." *Fortune*. Web. 9 Nov 2017.
[iii]"Women Representation On Fortune-500 Boards-Inches Upward." *Catalyst.Org.* Web 9 Nov 2017.
[iv] Barsh, J., & Yee, L. "Unlocking The Full Potential Of Women At Work." *McKinsey & Company*., (2012) Web. 28 Mar 2016.
[v] Barsh, J., & Yee, L. "Unlocking The Full Potential Of Women At Work." *McKinsey & Company*., (2012) Web. 28 Mar 2016.
[vi] Coffman, Julie. Neuenfeldt, Bill. "Everyday Moments of Truth: Frontline Managers Are Key To Women's Career Aspirations." *Bain and Company.* (Jun 2014). Web. 15 Aug 2015.
[vii] Hewlett, Sylvia. Green, Tai. *Center For Talent Innovation* (2015) Web. 20 Mar 2015.
[viii] Barsh, J., & Yee, L. "Unlocking The Full Potential Of Women At Work." *McKinsey & Company*., (2012). Web. 28 Mar 2016.
[ix] Washington State Department of Labor or Industries. *Workplace Bullying and Disruptive Behavior*. (2011). Web. 11 April 2016
[x] Dusen, A. (2008, Mar 24). "Ten Signs You're Being Bullied At Work." *Forbes*. Web. 11 Apr 2016
[xi] Namie, G. "2014 WBI Workplace Bullying Survey." *Workplace Bullying Institute*. Web. 16 Mar 2016.
[xii] Ely, R., Ibarra, H., & Kolb, D. "Women Rising: The Unseen Barriers." *Harvard Business School Publishing* (2013): n. pag. Web. 15 March 2016.
[xiii] Biernat, M., & Sesko, A. (Mar 2010) "Prototypes Of Race And Gender: The Invisibility Of Black Women." *Journal of Experimental Social Psychology*, Vol 46(2), 356-360. Web. 18 Mar 2016.
[xiv] Drexler, P., PhD. . (2014, Jul 28). "Both Men and Women Prefer Working For A Male Boss." *Psychology Today*. Web. 20 Oct 2017
[xv] Fapohunda, T. M. "Managing Workplace Bullying." *Journal of Human Resource Management. Vol. 1, No. 3, 2013, pp. 39-47.* Web. 20 Oct 2017
[xvi] Miller, Claire, C. "It's Not Just Fox: Why Women Don't Report Sexual Harassment." *New York Times* (April 2017). 23 Oct 2017.
[xvii] Feldblum, C., & Lipnic, V., (2016) Select Task Force on the Study of Harassment in the Workplace Report. *Equal Employment Opportunity Commission.*